Balance 20/20

Balance

20/20
SIX KEYS

**TO A
HARMONIOUS LIFE**

George Bartko

Red Wheel
Boston, MA / York Beach, ME

First published in 2004 by
Red Wheel/Weiser, LLC
York Beach, ME
With offices at:
368 Congress Street
Boston, MA 02210
www.redwheelweiser.com

Library of Congress Cataloging-in-Publication Data

Bartko, George.
  Balance 20/20 : six keys to a harmonious life / George Bartko.
    p. cm.
  ISBN 1-59003-043-5 (alk. paper)
  1. Conduct of life. I. Title: Balance 20/20. II. Title.
  BF637.C5B38 2004
  158.1—dc22
                        2004000704

Typeset in Fairfield Light by Gopa & Ted2, Inc.
Printed in the United States
Maple Vail

11 10 09 08 07 06 05 04

  8 7 6 5 4 3 2 1

The paper used in this publication meets the minimum requirements of the American National Standard for Information Sciences—Permanence of Paper for Printed Library Materials Z39.48-1992 (R1997).

I dedicate this book to my wife, Debbie, who is my soul mate, and my daughter, Giana, who is my angel. It is because of the both of you that I have this beautiful life that I live every day. No combination of words could ever truly express the deep love I have for you both.

Contents

Acknowledgments

Thank you to all of my family and friends
who continue to inspire and believe in me.

Debbie
Giana
Mom and Dad
Rosemarie and Suzanne
Scott and Ken
Sean, Tess, and Jack
Sue and Bob
Uncle George, Julie and Lou
Aunt Judy
Gram and Poppie
Anthony and Lisa
Phil and Robyn
Matthew and Ross
Ronnie and Judy
Frank (L1)
John and Pam
Peter R.
Ron and Colleen
Tommy and Patty, Nicole, and Michael
Wassim and Safa
Adriana, Rob, Chryssy, Gary
The Basketball Crew

Special acknowledgments go to Debbie for her support, assistance, creative cooking, and food styling; to Anthony for his words, support, criticism, and guidance; to Robyn Heisey for finding me, believing in my concept, and for giving me this tremendous opportunity; and to Caroline Pincus for connecting with this project and assisting in its direction.

More thanks to:
Danielle Chang
Gregg Bernard
Doyle Hunt
Dale and Susan Hamilton

Balance 20/20

Introduction:

WHAT *IS* LIFE BALANCE, ANYWAY?

JOHN LENNON once wrote, "Life is what happens to you when you're busy making other plans." So true, isn't it? Our lives often take turns almost in spite of us. We certainly don't feel in control. Everything moves so fast and everyone everywhere complains about not having enough time. So many of us feel out of balance, but do we know how to get off the hamster wheel? Too often the answer is no.

Our parents lived in a world that ran on different rules, and things simply didn't move as fast. Many of us can even remember what life was like before cell phones and pagers and e-mail and voice mail. For starters, we had more quiet in our lives, more time free of input, input, input. We also didn't often question if this was all there is.

My dad worked as a foreman on an assembly line and never missed a day of work in thirty-one years. His generation was built on this kind of work ethic, and he never for a minute thought there was any other way to live. He and my mother raised me to be a good worker, too: to get a good education, find a reputable company to work for, work hard, earn money, and maybe have some fun on the weekends. And for years that's just what I did. I didn't even give it much thought. That's just the way things were.

For twelve years I worked as the chief operating officer at a New York–based company. I loved my job and was successful at it, but I knew something was missing. I left my house every day at 7 AM and arrived home at 7 PM. My nights and weekends were filled with errand running, bill paying, and just getting everything done. As time passed, I saw the effects on my relationship with my wife and daughter and the rest of my family. And on myself. My family was getting the leftovers, and I wasn't spending time doing things that had deeper meaning, or for that matter, that I enjoyed.

I kept a personal to-do list of all the things that I would do *for myself* when things slowed down and life gave me more time. But then I came to the realization that such a day might never come and that my precious list was never going to get done unless I changed the way I approached life. I craved balance and realized that *I* was the only one who could make it happen.

I needed a plan and a new list of priorities. As a management guy, I figured that some of my management techniques could help me here, too. So I set out to develop a time management system that would allow me to live in balance with the natural, human-made, and spiritual elements of my life. My system is based on prioritizing what I call the Six Pillars of Life Balance (more on those in a moment) and finding time for all these things, not some time off in the future but today—in their proper balance, of course. After sharing my time management ideas with a broad circle of family and friends, it became clear to me that time management is *the key* to a life of balance. That's why it's the cornerstone of this book.

Living by my own Life Balance Plan, I now enjoy life like I never have before. I no longer feel so easily overwhelmed by life, and I have found ways to organize my time so that *I get to do the things that really matter to me*. I still work hard to provide for myself and my family, but I also have *time* for my daughter and my wife, I have *time* for my friends and my hobbies, *time* to be of service in the world, and *time* for myself. I wouldn't say I am a new person, but I do wake up every day with an inner fire to take on the game of life. I made it happen, and so can you.

Many people are shaken awake by extreme events, but you don't have to wait to be struck down by illness, a layoff, the threat of divorce, or the loss of a loved one to decide to evaluate your priorities and reshape your life along more sane lines. It's enough that you feel, as I did, that something is out of whack. The more proactive you become right now about reshaping your life to give it better balance, the more years you'll have to enjoy all the riches this life has to offer.

What's to Come

As I see it, there are six essential components to a life in balance. Taken together, they represent who we are and how we choose to be in the world. I call them The Six Pillars of Life Balance.

1. Connections

2. Mind

3. Motion

4. Spirit

5. Fuel

6. Business

The first pillar, **Connections**, refers to our relationships. Creating and maintaining quality relationships is the key to truly experiencing a sense of inner harmony. Relationships are like an emotional barometer. We feel up or down depending on the strength of our feeling of connection.

A healthy **Mind**, the second pillar, is more multifaceted. It's not just about intellect and knowledge but also creative expression and reflection. Once we're out of school, we tend to stop challenging our minds to continue learning and therefore turn off our intellectual spirit. Part of finding balance usually has to do with stimulating ourselves to learn new things. Allowing ourselves the outlet to *create* also expands our minds by giving us the ability to mesh knowledge with artistic vision. And finally, having a mind in balance always involves taking time out to quiet our thinking and allow for rejuvenation through reflection.

The third pillar, **Motion**, refers to our level of physical activity. Many of us work out for physical health, which, of course, is the foundation for all other aspects of life. But movement is also about connecting with spirit. It should be as natural as breathing. That's why it's so important to find ways of moving that you love, so it's not just a chore to keep you fit.

Spirituality, as I use the word, is not necessarily about being religious, although it may be for some people. Rather I think of spirit, the fourth pillar, as a sense of connection to the universe. Devoting some part of every day to an awareness of this connection—whether through prayer, meditation, lighting a candle, or walking in the park—is integral to a life of balance.

Fuel is the fifth pillar. The fuel we supply to our body is our strongest silent link to balance. Every thing we put in our mouths to eat influences our health. Without a well-fueled body, there is no balance. Of course it's tricky. Every day we hear about new nutritional dos and don'ts. The point is, you owe it to yourself to make informed choices about what you eat. And drink.

Although not a "natural" part of our world, I add **Business** as the final pillar because we all devote so much time to it, and in this day and age it's so much a part of who we are. And by business let me be clear that I mean both professional and personal business. It's important to evaluate what we do for work to be sure it's providing a rewarding experience, but it's just as important to have good systems for handling our personal banking, home, medical needs, insurance, auto, and so on, lest managing those areas become a full-time job.

Since making time for each of these pillars is key to living a life of balance, good time-management tools are essential. Chapter 1 sketches out the system I have developed that has been so successful in my life. The following chapters then look closely at each of the six pillars. Each of those chapters begins with a brief questionnaire to get you started. The idea with the questionnaires is not to get some ideal score, not to rate yourself, but just to figure out where you might want to reprioritize or refocus.

Once you have identified what's going on in these six areas and what you might want to do differently, the next step is to prioritize and make a Life Balance Plan, where you actually *schedule in time* for all six areas. And that's the key, because, as we all know, if we don't make time for each pillar, we simply won't *get* to the gym, *spend* time with our kids, *eat* those greens, and so on. Once you have a schedule that reflects your priorities, you have created a blueprint for achieving balance for life.

Of course unforeseen circumstances or events will inevitably alter this plan from time to time. You may not stick to every appointment, but you will *know* what you are missing or neglecting. Your Life Balance Plan will keep you in touch with your priorities and will be a continual reminder to get back on course. Superman is fiction, but if you expect the occasional deviation and then make sure to get yourself back on track, you will have success. If you keep the plan in effect and alter it along with your inevitably shifting priorities, then you will have found life balance.

Finally, lest you think I'm about to suggest that you quit your job and eat only rice and beans or anything so extreme, let me assure you that all I'm here to do is help *you* decide where you want to make adjustments and to give you some practical suggestions for how you might go about doing that. It's all about becoming more awake to where you may be missing out on living your own life.

The photographs you will find throughout the book were included as inspiration, to give you some nonverbal space for reflection and meditation. My hope is that you will let these photographs take your mind to a quieter, more introspective place as you look at your life and begin to shape your own Life Balance Plan.

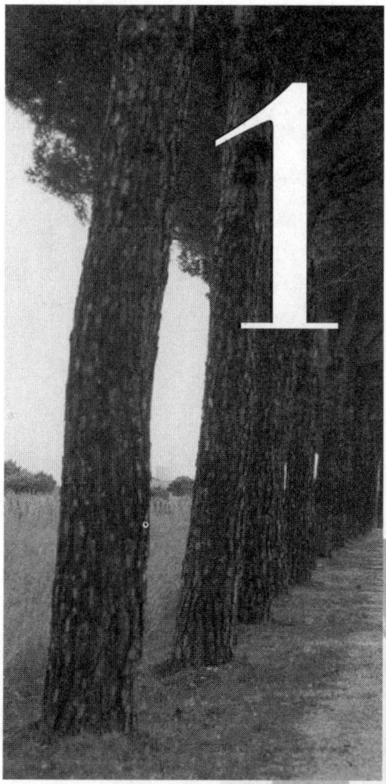

1 The Life Balance Time Management System

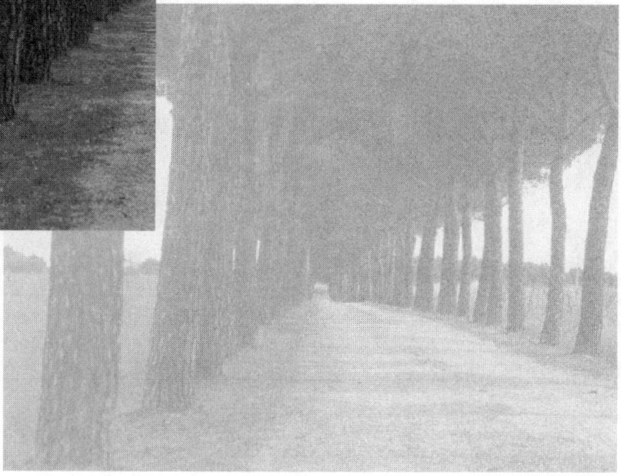

As I MENTIONED IN THE INTRODUCTION, time management is the cornerstone of my program for life balance. Without a sense of control over how we spend our time, we'll never have balance. Our human condition these days seems to involve feeling starved for time. We all feel it, but we don't seem to know what to do about it. Well, I've got some simple tools that can change all that for good.

The Life Balance Day Planner

The first thing I want you to do is get a day planner. Whether paper based or electronic, a day planner can keep track of all the details of your schedule and to-do lists and free your mind from having to store all the information you need to get through your day. It gives you the freedom to *experience* your life, not just run it.

For my system to work, it's important that your planner include the following:

- ▶ A calendar
- ▶ Task lists (date based)
- ▶ An address book
- ▶ A binder (in which to keep the planner)

THE CALENDAR

We have so many places to be in our lives. The best way to keep an organized and time-efficient schedule is to use an appointment calendar. It may seem obvious, but then again I'm always surprised at how many people *don't* use a calendar. I promise: If you start to use one,

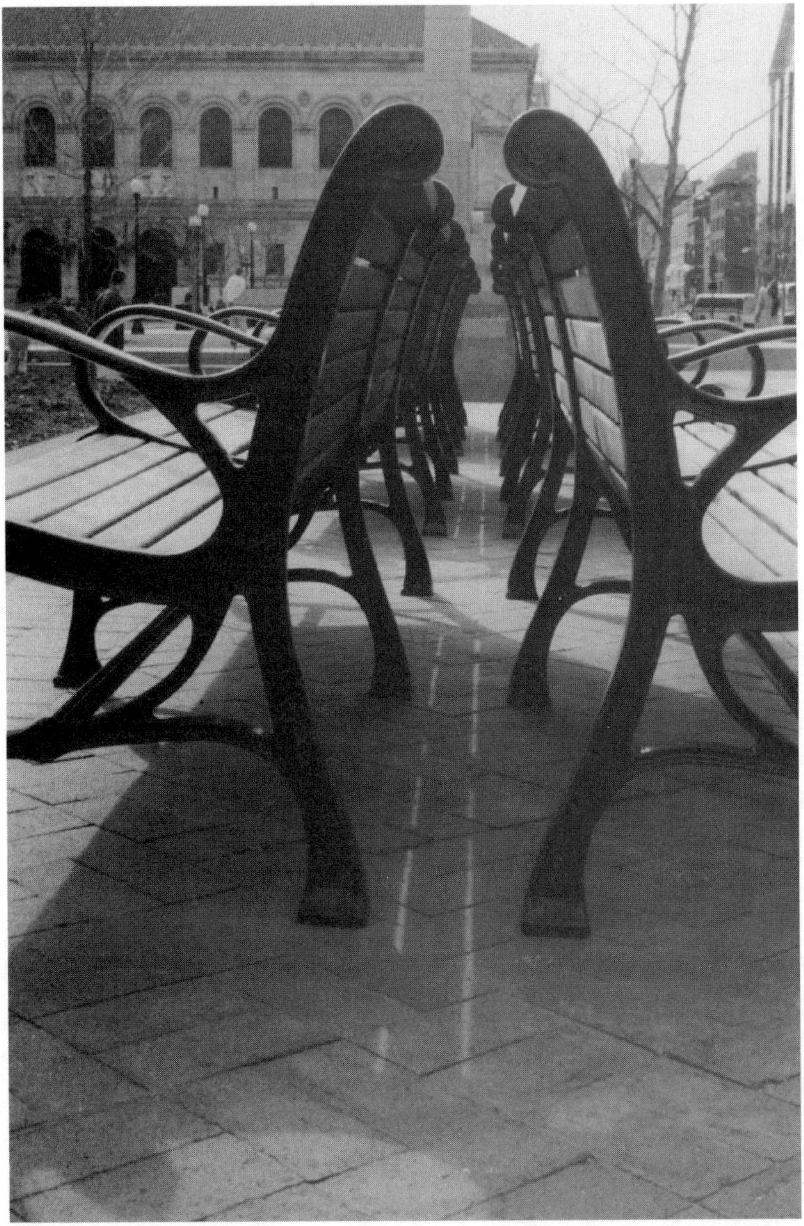

and use it properly, you will love it. If you tend to be late or miss appointments, you won't have any more excuses, but then again you won't be overwhelmed having to remember where to be when!

Many people know when they need to be somewhere but they neglect to factor in the time it will take to prepare and then get there. That's why I recommend scheduling every appointment with two entries: one for the time you need to be there and the other for the time you need to *leave* for the appointment. Thinking this through will save you lots of hassles. Enter *all* your recurring events, such as pillar activities (see chapters 2 through 7), birthdays, anniversaries, doctor checkups, visits to the gym, auto service, and inspections.

Electronic calendars will let you enter the info just once and then set the repeating dates or intervals. They will also let you set reminders in advance of an appointment. If you are using a paper calendar, you will need to do this manually, but you can still enter your repeating appointments, being sure to make an entry a few days or weeks in advance of the event to remind you to send a card, pick up a gift, make reservations, or anything else you may need to do to prepare for the appointment.

Tasks

Next up is the task list. We all have our quirky little systems for trying to remember the things we need to do—sticky notes, scraps of paper, writing on our hands, leaving ourselves voice mail. Centralizing your notes into one task list will vastly simplify the process for getting things done.

Create the task list with corresponding due dates. An electronic organizer does this easily. *No task* should be without a due date, because it seems to be human nature to leave undated tasks for that fantasy day in the future "when we have time," which is, of course, never. To complete your tasks, schedule them on a specific day. If you don't accomplish them, keep moving them to other dates. But never leave them hanging in space.

The Address Book

I suggest keeping one address book for both personal and business contacts. Electronic organizers allow you to categorize your addresses for easy access. Use the categories to relieve yourself from trying to remember the name of your plumber, electrician, or any other person with whom you have infrequent contact.

The Binder

The only way the day planner will work is if it's always with you and things don't get lost before you can get them organized. That's why it's important to keep it in a binder or something in which all of your paper items and your electronic planner will fit. It doesn't have to be big and heavy; you can use any size that's convenient for you. There are so many to choose from these days. I have a small, zippered binder that has a special pocket for my electronic organizer. If you carry a brief-case, backpack, or purse, find a binder that's small enough to fit inside it. The idea is to always have it available so you never need to put off scheduling an event or task.

Use your binder to carry receipts, prescriptions, claim checks, directions, business cards, or any other paper that you need quick access to that day. Be sure to clean it out every night and organize it for the next day.

The binder should also have a pen and note pad. Even in this electronic age paper is still critical because you may need to hand someone a written note.

How to Use Your Planner

Now comes the fun part—actually using your planner. I suggest that you begin and end your day by looking at your planner. Use the evening to organize and prioritize your appointments and task list. If you know your schedule for the next day, you will awaken with a clear sense of your day and a desire to complete your schedule. Use the morning as a review to get a mental picture of your day.

PRIORITIZING YOUR TASK LIST:
LIFE TASKS VS. BUSINESS TASKS

I divide my task list into two priority levels: life tasks and business tasks. Business tasks are the things we do to take care of life business: bill paying, job-related tasks, the laundry, shopping, and the like. Life tasks, on the other hand, are the things we do to enrich ourselves and align with the natural forces of our existence. Be sure to schedule all of your life tasks first and then schedule your business tasks. Business tasks will take all the time you allow them or they will somehow miraculously get done in the time you give them. When we put our business tasks first, with our life tasks only getting done "when we have time," we lose balance and focus. You don't want your life to be about *what you do,* but about *who you are.* This is the key concept in prioritizing your time. Also enter into your calendar those blocks of time when you're *not* available (i.e., times when you're needed at home with your kids) so you don't accidentally double-book yourself.

The goal is to be able to balance your time in all areas, but of course when one area requires more time, you will have to make choices. This is why it's so important to establish your priorities. These will become the basis for your balanced life, the foundation of your own personal mission statement. Only you can decide which things in *your* life can never be compromised and which can be rescheduled to later.

Making Your Life Plan

Of course, you must file your taxes, make your rent or mortgage payment, and go to work every day, but then there's the rest. Relationships, spirituality, nutrition, exercise, rest, creativity, and learning will not happen consistently unless you schedule them. So let's sit down and begin to make your life plan.

Number each of the Life Pillars from one to six, with one being the area that you will almost never let lapse and six being the area that could wait if it had to.

___ Connections

___ Mind

___ Motion

___ Fuel

___ Spirit

___ Business

Once you identify your priorities in these six areas, decisions are easily made. If you have health problems and they are related to your nutrition or physical state, then Fuel and Motion should become your top two priorities, because without health, the other aspects of your life may become irrelevant. If your family and friends are consistently neglected for your career, then you'll want to make Connections your highest priority (unless, of course, you don't mind living a lonely life).

Remember, until you organize your time, it will never belong to you. All those things you want to do with your time—take up photography, jog in your local park, see family and friends—schedule them now. All those projects that seem too daunting—find time for them in your schedule. Break them down into manageable parts, if you need to, but schedule them in. That's the only way you'll get them done.

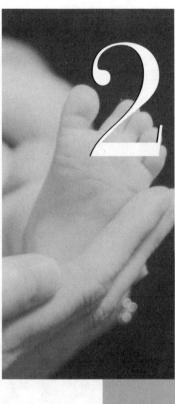

2

Connections—

CREATING AND MAINTAINING LOVING RELATIONSHIPS

RELATIONSHIPS COME FIRST because all our decisions, moods, and desires are regulated by our emotions, the most powerful of which is love. Love nourishes our soul and ignites the true feeling of being alive. It influences every aspect of who we are and gives us the foundation to treat everyone with respect and compassion. Creating and maintaining loving, connected relationships is essential to living a life in balance. The following Connections Test can be a good reality check for how balanced you are in the relationship department.

This and the other tests at the beginning of each of the following chapters are not meant to be an overall barometer of who you are, they are merely a starting point to help you begin the process of looking at your life differently. Answer the following questions with either A, B, or C. Then add up your score to see how well you are balancing life within this area.

THE CONNECTIONS TEST

A. Never = 1 point
B. Sometimes = 2 points
C. Always = 3 points

1. Do you regularly set aside time to call the most important person or people in your life? _____

2. Do you choose to be with family or friends over work or hobbies? _____

3. Do you make time to discuss emotional changes in the lives of the people closest to you? _____

4. Do you focus on giving more than receiving in your relationships? _____

5. When you are spending time with your family or friends do you shut off distractions such as television to focus solely on them? _____

6. Are you respectful and courteous to all people you interact with on a daily basis? _____

7. Are you caring and communicative when the people in your life are experiencing problems? _____

8. When you have a problem or an issue with someone, do you confront it immediately? _____

9. Do you let go of problems once they are resolved? _____

10. Do you praise people in your life for everyday achievements? _____

Scoring

Write your score next to each question number and then total.

1. _____
2. _____
3. _____
4. _____
5. _____
6. _____
7. _____
8. _____
9. _____
10. _____

Total: _____

Evaluation

10–15: It's time to reevaluate and take small steps to get on the path to achieving balance in this area.

16–20: You're on the path to balance in this pillar. Focus on your weak areas and you will take noticeable positive steps.

21–30: Congratulations! You're living at a high level of balance in this pillar. Determine the areas that will have the greatest impact on enhancing your life experiences.

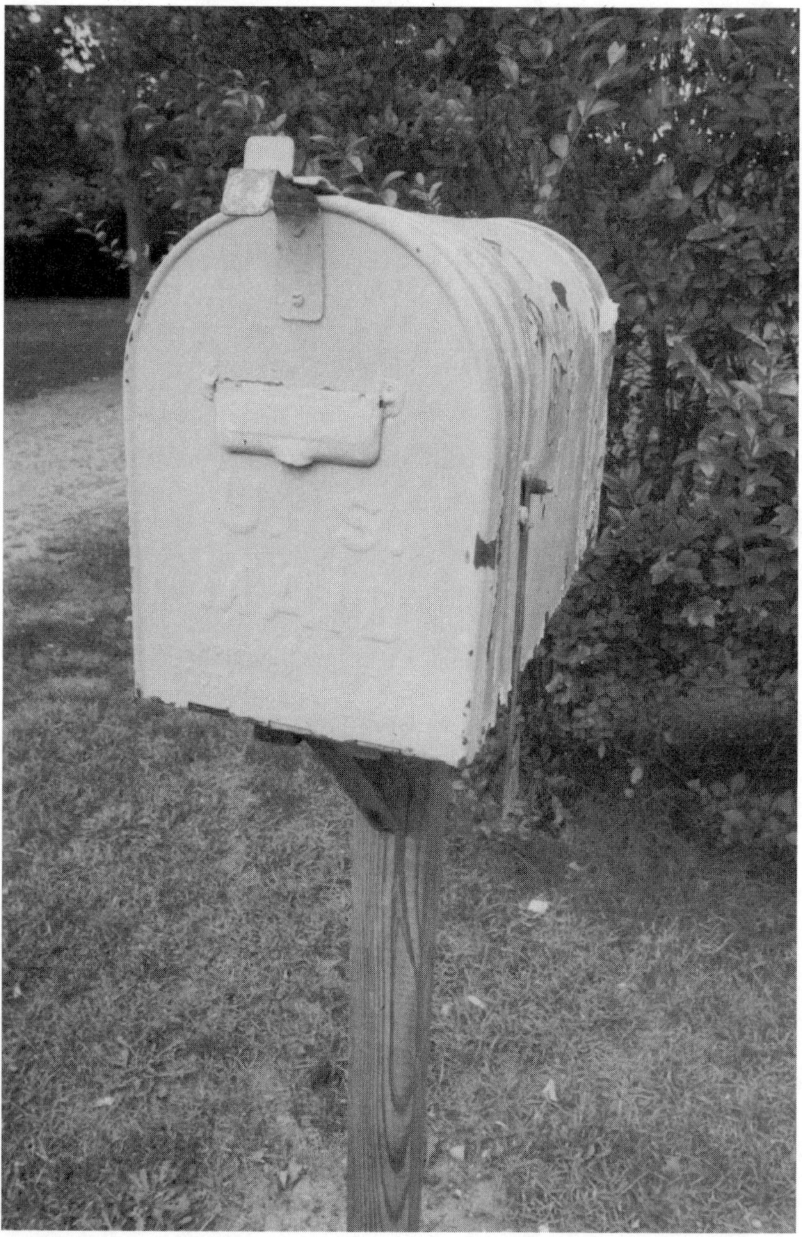

Are You the Best You Can Be?

Many of us split our priorities or water them down to the extent that no one and no thing is completely number one in our world. If your relationship to your job, your hobby, television, or any other nonhuman relationship is stronger than your relationships with people, then your connections are out of balance. If you are rich in possessions but relationship-poor, you will inevitably feel empty inside. One way to keep yourself on track is to ask yourself, every morning, *Am I the best romantic partner, spouse, parent, sibling, child, grandparent, friend, employee, manager, relative, and neighbor that I can be?* Think of all the important relationships in your life and ask this same question.

Whom Do You Love?

If you are in a romantic relationship, being the best partner is of paramount importance to your overall balance. Your mate should be a true partner, the person that you collaborate with in many aspects of your life. Complementing and building off each other should be the goal of any romantic relationship.

Of course your romantic relationship isn't the only important one. The love for parents, siblings, children, friends, and even coworkers may be a "different kind of love," but they are just as important. Parents and siblings bring a deep-rooted connection that you find comfort in because of the common history you share. If you are blessed with children, think back to the feelings you experienced at their birth. Do you continue to experience those feelings as they grow up? If not, you'll want to take a close look at why.

Close friends create an alliance and a therapeutic forum for voicing and working out your inner feelings. Coworkers and other professional relationships can also be a significant barometer of who you are as a person. In short, *every* person who crosses your path, no matter

how seemingly insignificant, should be treated with love—the love you naturally want to express as a member of this world.

How and Why We Get
Off Track with Our Partners

So why do our romantic relationships work so well in the beginning and then develop problems? Because these relationships are highly volatile. At the beginning we experience a rush of wonderful feelings, feelings that often relegate the rest of our existence—all other people, obligations, and desires—to trivial details. Nothing and no one is as important as this new person in our life. Our mind, body, and soul become consumed, and we get a natural, even obsessive high. At these times we are more attentive, more open to change, more accommodating than at any other time because the feelings we are experiencing overshadow reasons, opinions, habits, and other priorities.

These very responses by our emotional sensors actually cause most of the subsequent problems, neglect, and heartache experienced by many couples. People believe that this euphoria should be perpetual, but ultimately the feelings become less consuming. Once they do, we let the other areas of our life regain their importance and fill much of the space that was once exclusively reserved for our beloved. A life in balance means finding ways to capture those early emotions and sustain them throughout our life. Is it possible? Yes. But it takes a sustained commitment.

With Family

Many of us simply take for granted the love of family. Just as we do with romantic love, we tend to believe that our blood relationships don't need to be nurtured. Our love for our children often takes a similar course to our love for our mates. Having them gives us an initial rush of emotions, but soon after they become a relationship that requires attention and work. Some of us are inspired by the rewards parenting brings, and others are overwhelmed by the responsibility. The parent who is not the immediate caretaker can become disconnected, work and other interests getting in the way of a strong bond. It's easy to say, "There is always tomorrow." The truth is that you can never recover lost time with children. They grow up too fast, and the changes they go through don't wait for business trips or other interests to pass.

Ask yourself: I know what my daughter looks like, but do I really know who she is? Do I give my aging parents the attention they crave? Do my kids know me? *Nurture your connection with family.*

With Friends

The emotional relationships we develop with friends can be some of the most rewarding connections we have—supportive, therapeutic, unbiased, and just plain pure fun. Friends provide an emotional outlet that no one else can offer, because of their detachment from our immediate family and partner commitments. For this reason we must be very careful not to neglect them and treat them as bystanders to our lives; they are an integral part of our emotional health. Friends are not pets, there for our enjoyment when we want or need them. They require *our* attention to *their* matters as well. Perhaps you don't really have good friends these days. Many adults, especially men, don't. Think about what friends could mean to you and start cultivating your friendships today.

In Professional Relationships and with Acquaintances

Many of us spend a significant portion of our time with the people we work with. In fact, our colleagues often experience more of the "true us" than our family or friends do because they see us in many different lights—as a manager under pressure, perhaps as a collaborator on a project, doing public speaking, even playing on the company softball team. Additionally, you may hold significant influence over how they perceive *themselves* throughout their whole life, not just at work. We often don't tend to think of these relationships as important to our overall emotional happiness, but they are. That's why I urge you to cultivate healthy, respectful relations at work. Try to give the best of yourself at all times. Remember, even passing moments with your colleagues aren't easily forgotten.

Twelve Things You Can Do to Strengthen Connection

1. Just be nicer.

The first place to start is with a general commitment to being nicer to everyone in your life. Begin by just loving people more. Not just those close to you but everyone who crosses your path—other drivers, a customer, a sales clerk, even someone you simply pass on the street. Pay attention to how good it feels to be a caring human being. It raises the quality of all our lives. Not to mention that giving at a high level will come back to you in abundance.

2. Expect, accept, and manage change.

The dynamics established early in a relationship set up our expectations. We think that our partners should stay the same—as beautiful, as charming, as attentive—as they were in those first days. But everything changes, including your partner. Their inherent nature will remain the same, but their thinking, their desires, their appearance, and their goals will change. Can you accept that? If you knew that, would you have taken the risk of committing to a relationship with this person? Does knowing that add too much instability to your life? Well, if you want to be in a loving relationship, get over it.

The sooner you can accept that change will come, and with it an exciting challenge to evolve yourself and learn from it, the better off you will be. Many of us find this unnerving. We like routine and consistency. We don't want to change. If we have to be on our toes, we will never feel comfortable and settled in our relationships.

This is exactly the point. Comfort equals complacency, which yields indifference. We believe we have the right to let love "be" just because we "signed the contract." I am not saying that you shouldn't be comfortable with your partner. Of course that's important. What I am saying is don't let the comfort paralyze you. Expect that changes are coming, open yourself up to the challenge, and manage the changes by communicating and adapting to each other.

3. Remember that true love requires work.

Work may not be the right word. Everyone uses it, but what I mean is attentiveness, flexibility, and respect. If you tend to think a healthy relationship with a romantic interest, friend, or family member should be easy and you shouldn't have to work at it, think again. No relationship will be what you want it to be at all times. There will be periods

of change or simply moments when you become disconnected for any of a myriad of reasons. This is where you must truly have an open mind and heart and let go of personal egos and defensive walls.

Amy lived by the idea that true romantic love should be effortless. Once any of her romantic relationships became "hard" in any way, she just up and left, telling herself that it just wasn't the right one. She told herself, "Love should not be this hard." She just shuts people out of her life at the first sign of trouble. It's no wonder she has yet to find a stable relationship in any aspect of her life.

As hard as it can be, keeping our hearts open and avoiding the temptation to see troubled relationships as failures is how growth happens. Amy, like so many of us, avoided the kind of self-reflection that could have resolved her problem with intimacy. We all need to be alert to our emotional hot points and the issues that trigger difficulty, then communicate openly and honestly with others and make it our personal mission to overcome any obstacles that come up. Try to see problems as challenges and allow yourself to become inspired by the positive results that will result from your efforts.

There are times, of course, when two people are simply not right for each other. The initial physical attraction may not be enough to sustain a true connection. So it's important to know when to let romantic relationships go. But once you make a strong connection with someone and create a true partnership, know that there will be periods of growth and strain, and hang in there. Strong romantic partnerships are a precious gift that turn black-and-white into color.

4. Give your relationship a periodic performance review.

Most companies give their employees an annual performance review. Your relationships—all relationships in your life—will benefit infinitely from the same. You should schedule regular appointments to evaluate your relationships at least every three months. This practice often enables you to head off the problems I spoke about above by giving you the chance to be proactive when something seems amiss. By choosing a relatively short period of time between reviews, you can't get too far off track or disconnected beyond repair.

Reviewing a relationship may seem awkward at first until both of you become accustomed to opening up and sharing true feelings. And of course this will be extremely difficult if tough words need to be spoken. The one absolute rule you must have in these meetings is a commitment to honesty. If you hide your true feelings you will never fix, heal, and move on from difficult times.

Remember, this is for the benefit of both of you. Discuss goals, desires, physical needs, and whether you are making enough time for each other. Use this meeting to discuss and manage change in your lives. Ask what has changed in each of you and how these changes affect each one. Don't ignore the emotional fluctuations that we all naturally experience. And please try to avoid being defensive. It won't help to start the conversation with "You don't even know who I am. I am not the same person anymore."

▶ Listen, don't just hear.

During these periodic reviews, be sure to listen. Sure, that sounds easy, but listening is much more than hearing. Listen to what the other person's heart is saying. Give them real permission to let their innermost feelings pour out. Even if you do not agree with what they're saying, be sensitive to the fact that their feelings are true for them. In relationships, perceptions are far more important than "facts."

▶ Use the time for positive confrontation.

Many of us would rather do pretty much anything else than confront each other, but these evaluation meetings only work when you're willing to do that. There is nothing better left for tomorrow. Tomorrow usually turns into the next day and then never, and the time that passes can create perspectives and conclusions that were never meant to be, unnecessarily widening the emotional gap in the relationship. You will be amazed at how productive you can feel and how much you can accomplish in life, especially in your emotional life, if you deal with issues immediately.

5. Let it go.

Another important aspect in balancing your connections is the ability to truly forgive. Forgiving requires open communication. If either person is not completely forthcoming, the issue will linger and create secret resentment. Resolving the conflict at the time you are discussing it means you can *let it go*. Time is precious. Spend it on positive feelings and creating harmonious love. Follow this in every relationship and the emotional weights will be lifted off your shoulders. Whatever you can do to diminish resentment in your life will only help open up doors to deeply rewarding relationships.

Another area where we tend to cling to our anger—mainly to our own detriment—is in day-to-day interactions with the strangers that cross our path. Someone cuts us off on the highway or shortchanges us at the store and we're all too quick to boil over. And who is really harmed by our anger? We harm ourselves!

I urge you to take the time to think through your reactions. Do some deep breathing and let it go. These people don't even know you, and chances are they will forget the incident within seconds, if they even registered it at all. Having the ability to let things go allows you to keep from accumulating negative feelings in your own mind and soul. People make mistakes. They may be experiencing difficult times in their life.

Understanding this will free you from feeling personally attacked. Live every moment at the highest level of love you can and you will experience balanced connections with others.

6. Don't ask for more than the other person can give.

As I mentioned earlier, our inherent nature doesn't change over time. Too often I see people demanding things of others that they themselves may be capable of without accepting the fact that the other person may not have this same ability. We are all born with and acquire a set of "tools" that gives us the ability to handle situations a certain way. We must realize that we don't all have the same set of tools and stop trying to force others into giving more than they are capable of.

Let me be clear. I am not suggesting that we should make excuses for people's actions or let them off the hook for acting inappropriately. Rather I am saying that we have to know when to stop putting a square peg in a round hole and focus our energy on playing to people's strengths. You need to assess whether you are reaching the other person and know when you've reached the limit of their ability to "see" your point.

7. Participate.

We have become a society of takers, always asking, "What can you do for me?" instead of "What can I do for you?" One of the most important elements to achieving balance in your relationships is to "be the highest giver." If you give in relationships, you will receive so much more in return. I do not mean material giving; I mean giving of your time, support, friendship, guidance, and love.

John was the personnel director of a large law firm and the father of two, Jake and Laura, who were six and three. His wife, Lois, also worked full-time, and the children were left with a babysitter five days a week until one of them returned home, which was usually no earlier than 6 PM. John worked for the firm for twenty years and made a very good salary. Lois made a similar salary, but combined they made just enough to make the bills. John and Lois finally decided that it was too much. The kids needed a full-time parent. They could cut back on certain areas of their life and make it work on Lois's income, but they were not going to cut back on their children. And so John quit his job.

Part of living in balanced connection is taking a proactive role in your relationships, spending quality time with the immediate people in your life. Time in the same room is not time together. Turn off the television and just talk and listen. Look at the interests of those around you and see if you can join in. Inject your personality and time into the experiences of the people in your life and you will become part of the fabric that makes up their life.

The best way to stay proactive in your relationships is to schedule regular activities together that cannot be rescheduled, interrupted, or postponed. Find things you all like to do, such as a movie night or an early morning bike ride, and decide on certain days and times for these shared activities that fit everyone's schedule. Then set them up as recurring appointments in your planner. These can be weekly, bimonthly, monthly—whatever works for both or all of you. Remember this applies to relationships with parents, friends, siblings, partners, relatives, and children. You will be thankful having a scheduled event to keep you on course with those closest to you.

By participating like this and always giving committed love to those around you, you will build an emotional empire. Be sure to find things to do that your schedule can accommodate. I have a two-year-old daughter, and no matter what my day is like, I always put her to bed. My schedule allows for this. We take that time to be together and to be thankful for all that we have.

8. Touch.

In our closest relationships, it is important to balance a physical connection as well. There is nothing more elevating than a healthy physical relationship. I don't necessarily mean sex, but time alone together to be sensual. Nonsexual touch with children, parents, siblings, and friends is an equally important way of connecting. If you ignore the body's desire for touch, you will be depleting yet another sensor that contributes to your emotional well-being. Touching, hugging, and massaging engage our physical love, which is the complement to our emotional love. Keeping both components active will strengthen the bond between you and will allow you to experience the highest level of romantic love.

9. Give all that is free.

Elizabeth has a hard time expressing her love for the people around her and rarely spends time with them. When she does show up, she is carrying gifts for everyone.

She is obsessed with buying people gifts. Every moment is a reason to give something. She pressures herself to go out and get the gifts; the reason behind them is secondary. The recipients always feel outdone and consequently feel pressure to reciprocate. No one is getting pleasure from the giving or receiving. This is not a healthy picture.

Giving of yourself—your time, your talents, your wisdom—is one of the best ways of keeping your connections strong. Of course you want to feel balance and not always be the giver, but giving of yourself is usually its own reward. Gift giving is not enough. You cannot cover up your lack of availability with presents or money.

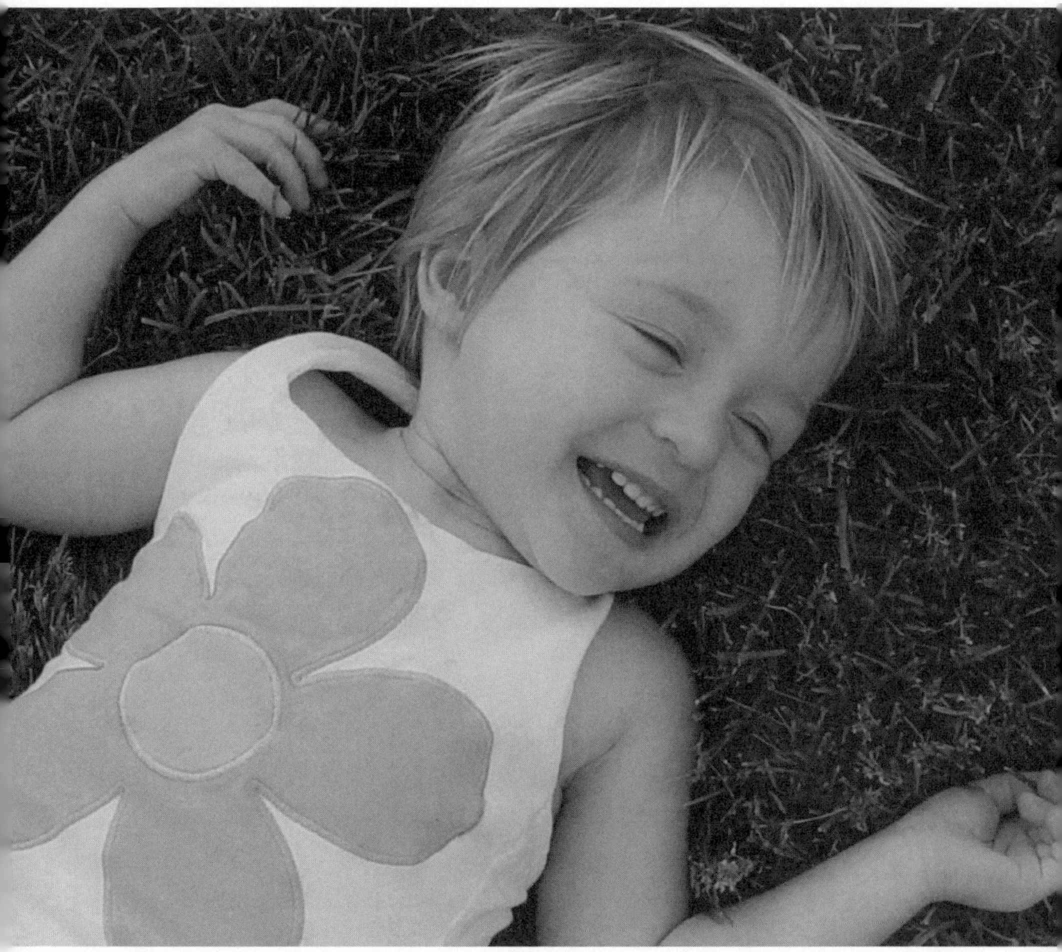

10. Reinvent love.

Love also needs to be reinvented from time to time. Relationships can get stale and in need of refreshing, which takes us back to point number 2 and the idea of managing change in your romantic life. Find ways to enhance the mood and inspire the time you spend not only with your mate but also with the other important relationships in your life. Be creative and look outside your normal routines. If your only "date" with your partner, friends, or family is going out to dinner, then set a recurring night out and alternate the responsibility for picking the activity and place. Set a rule that says you cannot do an exact repeat of a date, so that you spark creative interest in each other and the relationship. This will begin the process of reinventing love.

11. Find time for praise.

As a manager I believe that nothing enhances the quality of performance better than recognizing someone for good work. The same applies to your relationships. Be cognizant of the effort and achievements made by the people around you. Recognize even the smallest successes. Take every opportunity to build a person's morale. These are the actions that will be remembered. These are the things that motivate and energize and enhance the quality of life.

12. Don't forget about you.

Don't forget to have a loving relationship with yourself. Make time to reconnect with who you are and what you want in life. You should set aside time to evaluate your own goals and desires and see if you are following a life plan that is getting you there. Avoid that morning when you wake up and realize that your life has taken you on a path that you didn't intend to take. You are in control. Step back every now and then and look at the means you are following to get where you want to go.

Parting Words

▶ Surround yourself with the people you love and make the conscious commitment to be an active participant in their lives.
▶ Make your life easier by using your planner to manage the time spent on your relationships and they will never be neglected.

The following are some additional tips for creating balanced connections. They are meant to be points of departure, not assignments. Try these, make up your own—the point is, do it! Balanced connections will make you the richest person you can be.

Simple Activities That Build Connections

▶ Take the daily test. Ask yourself if you are the best romantic partner, spouse, parent, sibling, child, grandparent, friend, employee, manager, relative, and neighbor you can be. If not, make one simple change today toward being the best.

▶ Write a letter to someone you care about and tell him or her how much he or she means to you.

▶ Keep a journal of the most important people in your life. Interview them and use a video camera or audio recorder, or simply write it down. Interview your parents, children, siblings, and friends. Find out about significant events, their proud achievements, fears, love, regrets, and dreams. You will be rewarded with a deeper awareness of who they truly are.

▶ Make a photo album with pictures of the most important people in your life. Call it "My World" and leave it out and visibly accessible to you and visitors. Choose photos that truly depict who these people are to you. Browse through it every now and then and be reminded—in your heart—of how rich life is with these people in it, including those who influenced you but have passed on.

▶ Create a family tree. Use paper or software and go to online sources to try to find your history. Documenting family history gives you a deeper sense of your roots and something valuable to pass on to your children.

▶ Give a gift of time and place. The next time a gift is called for, arrange to spend time with the person instead. Give a card suggesting a specific time, place, and activity.

▶ Set up a regular time each week to call your family and friends. Just a catch-up call to stay connected.

▶ Make a life plan journal. Write down your goals for your relationships and every other area of your life. Refer to it every year on your birthday to see if you are following your plans.

▶ Have an evaluation day. Schedule a recurring appointment with your romantic partner, your family members, and your friends to evaluate your relationship in the following areas:

○ Goals

○ Attentiveness

○ Needs

○ Caring

○ Spending quality time

○ Change

○ Problems/issues

▶ Spend one day being nice to *everyone* you meet. Be conscious of every interaction and treat people as you would want to be treated. See how good that feels.

▶ Take a day off from work, televisions, or any other activity to be with someone you love.

▶ Have a friend night or vacation. Taking time away to be with friends is an important time for you and them.

▶ Plan a let-it-go day. Spend the day reconciling all issues with people in your life so you can move on.

▶ Plan for physical romance. Yes, in this hectic world of ours it can help to schedule time for romantic connection. Give a massage, make love, or just spend quiet time touching.

▶ Reinvent. Pick a relationship that may have become stale and devise a plan to give it new life.

▶ Plan a party. Bring together as many important people as you can to celebrate their influence in your life.

▶ Eliminate. As important as it is to surround yourself with the best people in your life, it is equally important to know when someone is draining you. Take a day to say goodbye to that person.

▶ Praise someone in your life for a small accomplishment. It could be as simple as saying "You are the best mother" or "Thanks for caring for me so much."

3 Mind—

STIMULATING THE INTELLECT, CULTIVATING CREATIVITY, AND DEVELOPING YOUR POWER OF REFLECTION

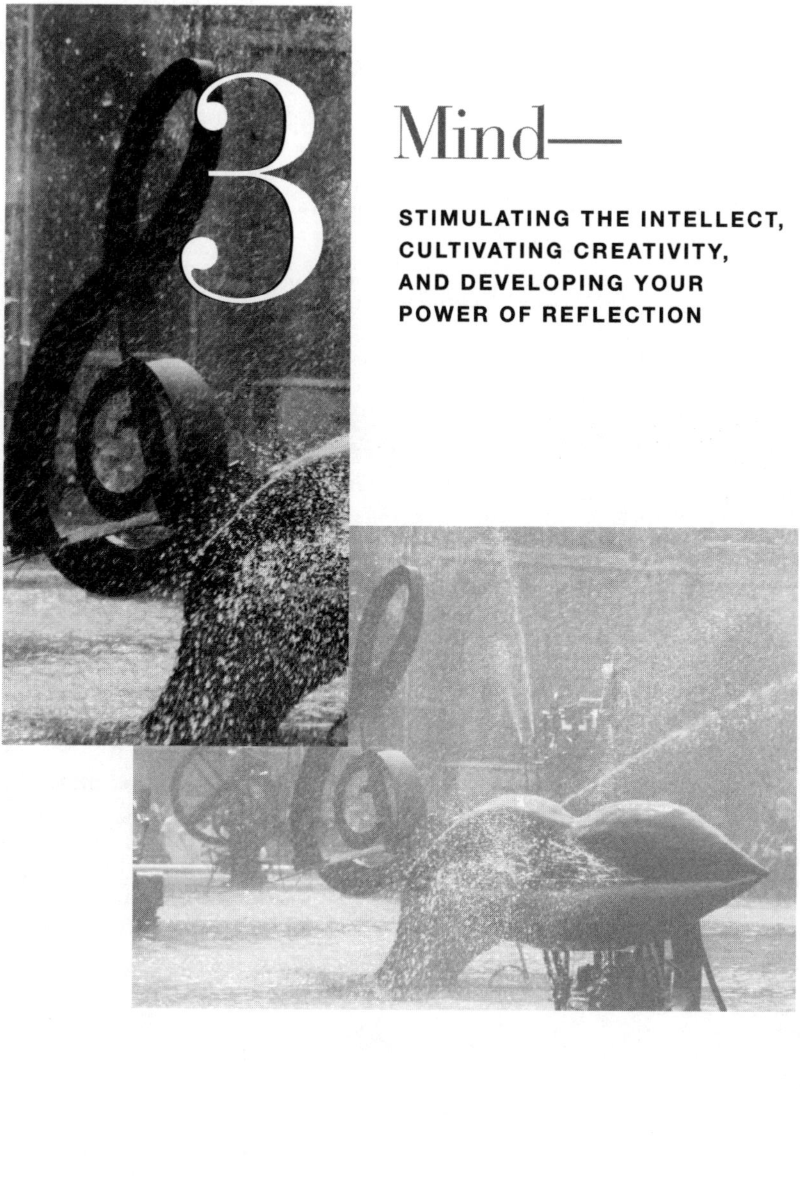

THE MIND TEST

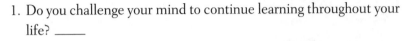

A. Never = 1 point
B. Sometimes = 2 points
C. Always = 3 points

1. Do you challenge your mind to continue learning throughout your life? _____

2. Do you have a mental or physical list of subjects that you are interested in learning about? _____

3. Do you take classes on subjects that interest you? _____

4. Do you choose books or movies based on the knowledge you will gain from them? _____

5. When faced with a challenging mental task, do you make time to work it out? _____

6. Do you have a mental or physical list of activities that stimulate your creative spirit? _____

7. Do you utilize a set time to perform creative activities? _____

8. Do you attend exhibits or shows that complement your creative interests? _____

9. Do you have a set time to slow down your thoughts and quiet the constant barrage of life? _____

10. Do you perform activities without background distractions such as television or music? _____

SCORING

Write your score next to each question number and then total.

1. _____

2. _____

3. _____

4. _____

5. _____

6. _____

7. _____

8. _____

9. _____

10. _____

Total: _____

EVALUATION

10–15: It's time to reevaluate and take small steps to get on the path to achieving balance in this area.

16–20: You're on the path to balance in this pillar. Focus on your weak areas and you will take noticeable positive steps.

21–30: Congratulations! You're living at a high level of balance in this pillar. Determine the areas that will have the greatest impact on enhancing your life experiences.

Children absorb every subject that crosses their path. They constantly ask "why?" because they are hungry for knowledge. After we leave school many of us treat our minds like archives where knowledge is stored, not a place that is called upon continually to expand. As adults we tend to lose this enthusiasm because life gets in the way and we tell ourselves we don't have time to learn anymore. Can you remember the last time you actually studied something that was not related to your profession?

Of course a healthy balanced mind is about more than just acquiring knowledge. It is also about nurturing your creativity and using your capacity for reflection. These three areas, when balanced, will round out and exercise the full power of your mind. Let's look at each area closely.

Life 101: Stimulating the Intellect

Miles is forty-five years old and works at an Italian restaurant that prides itself on its authentic cuisine and presentation. He wanted to be more involved and to feel that he was contributing to the overall customer experience. He decided to take an Italian course at night. He now serves the meals by their Italian names, pronounces the wines correctly, and can converse with customers who speak Italian.

When I was in high school my ambition was to get good grades. I studied for tests, not for knowledge. I did well, but did little to retain substantial information. There is so much to the world we live in, and to think about going through life without understanding it made me feel cheated. I had so much information at my fingertips, yet every day I ignored the chance to learn about it. History, astronomy, literature, foreign languages, and so many other areas were passing me by. But I decided that it's never too late to go back and learn about subjects I am interested in. Right now I am studying American History.

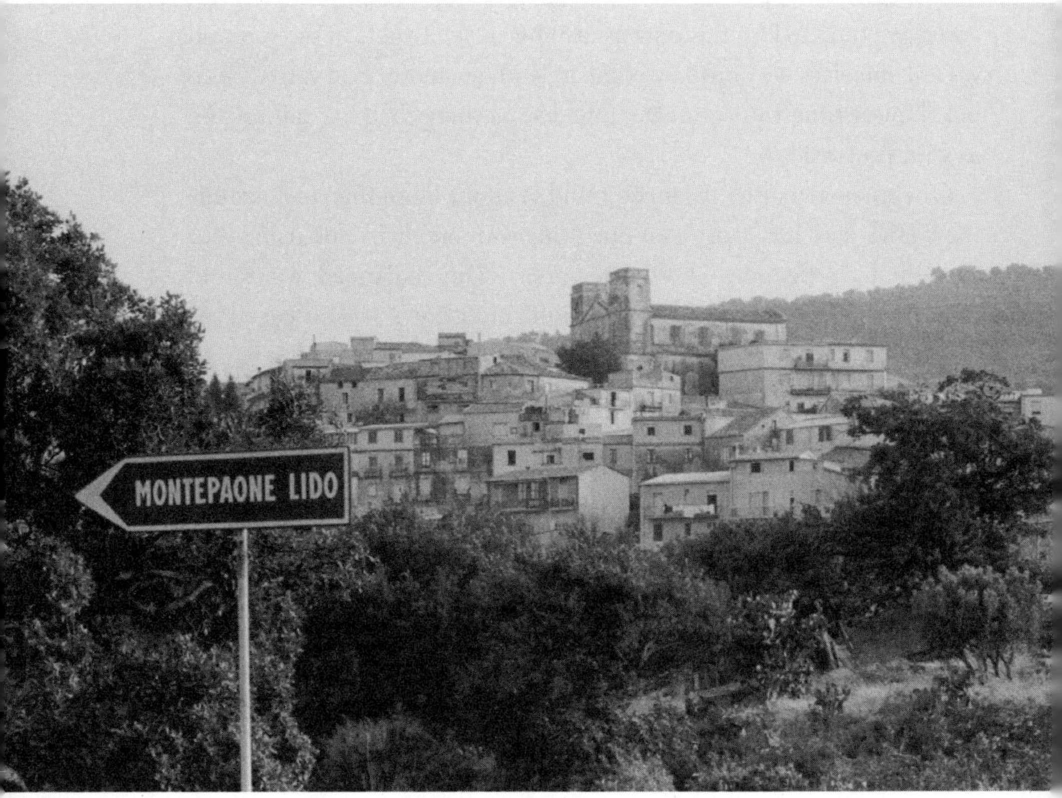
MONTEPAONE LIDO

Just think about it. Unlike when we were in school, now we get to learn new things purely for our own enjoyment.

Our intellect needs nourishment, just as our body does. Without this "nourishment" it loses its resiliency, its ability to grow. Its capabilities are literally diminished with lack of use. We need to challenge our minds continually, treating life as a constant adventure of discovery. We all have interests to explore; it's just that we lose the desire because we let the weight of everyday life consume our time. It's easy to say "I'm too tired or too busy." Instead, we can choose to cultivate that childhood yearning to know "why."

Don't allow yourself to be a bystander to the world and shut off a channel to some of the most awesome colors of life. Be an intellectual participant. Engage in deep learning experiences that challenge your mind to discover, question, associate, and assimilate new information. That's what balance is all about.

There are so many ways to stimulate the intellect. Just go out and see what sparks your interest. Here are a few suggestions to get you started:

20/20 Vision —

Activities to Stimulate Your Intellect

▶ Learn a foreign language. If you travel or would like to travel to foreign places there is nothing more rewarding than understanding and communicating with the people. You can learn through books, tapes, or classes.

▶ Study an event in history. By picking a single event you can take small steps into this area and see whether it drives your interest.

▶ Read books. Any books, any subjects, fiction or non-. Reading gives you time alone to wind down and to discover subjects, teachings, perspectives, and entertainment. Consider books on tape if you find reading tedious.

▶ Take courses or seminars. Your local colleges offer noncredit courses. Seminars on home buying/selling, gardening, investing, and automotive repair are always accessible.

▶ Rent movies. Choose movies that focus on an event in history, science, space travel, or biographies. This is a way to learn about events through an entertaining medium.

▶ Subscribe to special interest channels. All cable and satellite operators offer packages that have history, home repairs, or science channels that deliver endless hours of knowledge right to your home.

- Learn the computer. Many people do not know the basics. Even if you are self-taught, a basic computer class can be extremely beneficial to your ongoing growth in computer skills.

- Use the Internet. It's the best tool around for gathering information. Look up categories and go to university Web sites and preview course curricula for ideas.

- Think back to high school and see if there were subjects you wished you could remember or had pursued.

- Go to the bookstore and browse the aisles.

- Understand medicine. All of us will be faced with medical decisions throughout our lives, either for our body or for someone close to us. I'm not suggesting getting a medical degree, but there are many medical Web sites or books that offer basic information to help you gain perspective on the choices you need to make. Don't take any one person's advice. You need to be a mild expert in many areas.

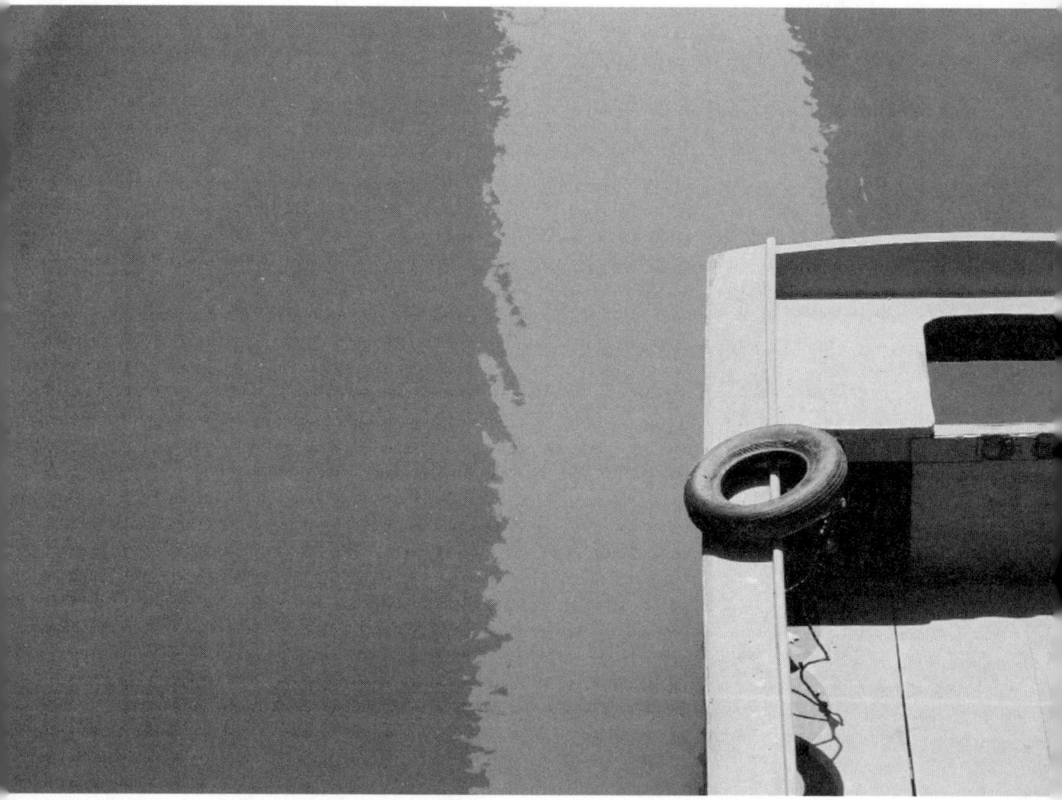

The Inspired Mind: Cultivating Creativity

Morgan was thirty years old and had worked in the same bank for ten years. Her intellectual stimulation was coming from learning international banking, but she felt closed off to something in her life. She decided to take an acting class because it was something she always felt she wanted to do. She watched movies and studied the acting in such a way that she felt it was time to give it a shot. The class pushed her in ways that she never thought she could go. She was not very outgoing and feared public speaking. The acting class became her coming out party, as she had to express her deepest emotions in front of a group. Her new mode of creative expression has balanced her work and desires and has helped her to become a different person in all aspects of her professional and personal life.

As important as cultivating the intellect is having an outlet that allows your mind to exercise its desire to express itself creatively. We can think and make decisions from pure intellectual knowledge, but by activating the creative side of our being we give a multidimensional approach to our lives and decisions, and they're always richer for it. Whether you love to cook, sing in your car, or take nature photos, you have a creative side that is always seeking expression.

Being creative doesn't mean that you have to be a professional artist, it just means being good enough to satisfy yourself. Your creativity is for no one but you; it should take your mind to a different place, a world that you can get lost in. If you don't have an outlet for your creativity, think about what you love—music, dance, food, color, drawing. Go out and explore different creative media. Let the search for balance take you on a true journey through the arts to find inspiration to feed your mind and soul.

Everything you do has a creative element to it. Imagine using your creativity even under the most ordinary circumstances. If you have to make a business presentation, try delivering it in a visually interesting way. Or take your kid's birthday. It's all about the show. If it doesn't stay interesting, you will lose your audience quickly. For example, instead of just playing musical chairs, try "Blackout Musical Chairs." Before you start the game, shut the lights and give everyone a flashlight. Kids love that kind of twist on things. I could give thousands of examples of using your creativity day to day. Send a greeting card to someone simply because you like its creative vision. The next time you serve dinner, garnish the plate. The point is, if you continually practice being creative, you can call on it when it is needed.

Here are a few suggested creative activities. Of course in this realm the sky really is the limit:

Activities to Cultivate Your Creativity

▶ Make your birthday gifts. Next time you need a gift for someone, try making something. It will be far more meaningful to the person, signaling that they mean enough to you to warrant using your creative juice. Here are some suggestions:

  ○ Make a collage of meaningful pictures of the recipient and you and have it mounted and framed.

  ○ Find a beautiful blank book and make a scrapbook of meaningful memorabilia.

  ○ Create and deliver a flower arrangement.

  ○ Make a video birthday card containing interviews with the recipient's friends and family, recalling their funniest moments with him/her.

▶ Start cooking. Take a cooking class or buy cookbooks that interest you and try teaching yourself. It will satisfy your mind, creativity, and nutrition—a bonus activity.

▶ Learn to throw pots. Take a pottery class or learn to do it at home.

▶ Take a painting class. Or just start painting on your own. Go to an artist supply shop and ask for help on the items you will need to get started.

▶ Learn to play a musical instrument. Take lessons or try it yourself with the help of a beginner's guide.

▶ Expand your musical horizons. Many of us get locked into one or just a few musical styles and never expose ourselves to alternative sounds. Spend several hours at a record store or at an online music Web site and experiment with different kinds of music.

Give yourself over to listening and see how your body and mind react to different sounds. Notice which musical styles motivate or calm you, and remember these for those times when you need to be brought up or down.

▶ Become a photographer. Take a photography course or buy a photography book and just get out in the world and start taking pictures of people or places that are meaningful to you. With digital cameras you can make mistakes and it won't cost you anything.

▶ Garden inside and out. Take a gardening course or buy a gardening book and look to work both in your home and outside. The diversity will keep you going on rainy days.

▶ Join a museum club and take advantage of lectures, shows, and programs.

▶ Take a writing class or begin writing on your own. Poems, short stories, or screenplays. Whatever motivates you.

Just follow your heart. Do whatever inspires you (provided it does no harm to others). Just know that allowing yourself to grow creatively is one of the great gifts of balance you can give yourself.

Silence Is Golden:
Developing Your Power of Reflection

With so much going on in our lives our minds can simply become over-loaded. We have conditioned ourselves to live with endless noise inside our brain. We tend to fill up every silent moment with sound. We watch TV; listen to the radio; or read something during breakfast, lunch, and dinner. We treat waiting—for a doctor, a train ride, or in line at the grocery store—as a chance to feed the frenzy in our heads. We find it harder and harder to just be in the moment and appreciate it for what it is. Silence is too "loud" for us. Constant distraction stifles our active thinking and creativity and prevents us from reflecting on who we are, why we are here, where we have been, and where we are going.

If we took more time to think about our lives, we would be more in control of our destiny. Many of us use medications to help us deal with our issues. There are times when these interventions are necessary, but many of us are too quick to turn there before trying other tools. It is difficult to face our own situations, but if we make a concerted effort to create quiet time in our lives, we can use it to reflect and review our situations and goals. This practice can help you build an inner strength that you can call on to make difficult decisions or to keep your life plan in effect. Please don't be afraid to hear your own thoughts. Use quiet down time to affirm or alter the path you are on.

I take the end of the day, as I sit with my daughter before she goes to bed, to reflect on all of the goodness and people in my life. She drinks her milk, and I sit and think. It is my quiet time to take an inventory of my situation and to slow down my thoughts. It becomes a renewal for my mind and spirit, and my priorities come back into focus. Leave yourself space like this on a daily basis and you will become centered in all that is good and positive, and it will help you to focus on the essential elements in your life.

20/20 Vision —

ACTIVITIES THAT QUIET YOUR MIND

Here are some ideas for taking a time out:

▶ Eat a meal alone and disconnect from the media.

▶ Take a walk in a quiet place. No cars or people.

▶ On your next drive alone turn off the radio.

▶ Do a chore—housework, gardening, anything—without any background noise.

▶ Before you go to bed, in the shower or bath, during your drive to work, or on the train, take time to reflect on your condition and situation.

▶ Take a day or two away from everything and everyone and reflect on where you are in time and space. Am I making a difference? Am I happy? You know the answer can be yes. You don't always have to be searching for something. Perhaps raising a family and being a loving spouse is enough. Maybe you've already achieved what you've set out to achieve but have never taken a moment to appreciate what you have.

Parting Words

► Remember, reflective time only happens if you schedule it into your life. Use your planner and set aside days and/or hours just for cultivating the powers of mind.

► Stretch your intellect. It will leave you with a youthful exuberance toward the world instead of the dead-end feeling of repetitive routines that require no thought at all.

► Look to find some mode of imaginative thought to exercise your creativity. Creative expression will motivate you for all aspects of life because it taps into the inspirational side of your being.

► Make time for quiet reflection and reduce the fury that we have created in our overstimulating world. Allow yourself to live with the constant flow of energy that comes with this mindful balance.

4

Motion—

**KEEP IT GOING, TAKE A BREAK,
AND MAKE TIME FOR YOU**

THE MOTION TEST

A. Never = 1 point
B. Sometimes = 2 points
C. Always = 3 points

1. Do you wake up every day feeling the need to perform some physical activity? _____

2. Do you choose stairs or walking over motorized alternatives? _____

3. Do you set aside time on a regular basis for physical activities? _____

4. Do you see a health professional to assess your overall physical well-being on a regular basis? _____

5. Do you have a strength training routine? _____

6. Do you find pleasure in moving your body? _____

7. Do you make time to meditate or to do nothing but relax? _____

8. Do you wake up feeling rested? _____

9. Do you make time for play—something you love to do? _____

10. Do you make time to pamper your body? _____

SCORING

Write your score next to each question number and then total.

1. _____

2. _____

3. _____

4. _____

5. _____

6. _____

7. _____

8. _____

9. _____

10. _____

Total:_____

EVALUATION

10–15: It's time to reevaluate and take small steps to get on the path to achieving balance in this area.

16–20: You're on the path to balance in this pillar. Focus on your weak areas and you will take noticeable positive steps.

21–30: Congratulations! You're living at a high level of balance in this pillar. Determine the areas that will have the greatest impact on enhancing your life experiences.

Is Your Body the Temple of Doom?

Stephen was always a regular at the gym. He played softball, bicycled every now and then, and participated in a regular game of basketball. Then he took on a difficult job that demanded tremendous brainpower, and his wife became pregnant. Life got in the way, and exercise went from high on his list to last on his list to off his list. Now he's thirty-seven and has not exercised in the last five years. He has become heavier than his normal weight and looks less energetic, and his easygoing way has disappeared. When regular exercise was a part of who he was, he was a different person. His mindset has narrowed, and his enthusiasm for life has been reduced to complaining about everything.

Have you become inert—tired and physically uninspired? Do you stand in the bathroom mirror and not recognize who is staring back at you? Did you skip your last high school reunion or do you fear running into someone from your past because you have "let yourself go"? The truth is, in many ways our physical body *is* a visual representation of who we are. It's time to let go of the excuses, forget about the past, and look forward. Our bodies were not created to sit on a couch, watch TV, and eat junk food. Nothing profound here, just the point that you need to balance a healthy mind and spirit with a healthy body.

When we were growing up we had a natural inclination to burn off energy through physical activity. You were probably one of those kids with boundless energy who ran your mother ragged. Or maybe you liked to wrestle, climb trees, play team sports, whatever. If you have lost that natural love of movement, it's time to reclaim it. Staying physically active will keep you young at heart, energetic, and fit. All part of a life in balance.

Of course it's just as important to rest, relax, and do things just for pleasure. We all need that kind of down time to refuel. In the following sections, we'll look at both aspects of the Motion picture.

Keep On Moving

> Tim is fifty years old and a solid 195-pound man. He looks good, but doesn't exercise, and he eats mostly unhealthy meals. He has a unique plan to manage his health. He uses a yearly doctor visit and full body scan to assess his level of "unhealthiness." His arteries are blocked but have not yet reached the "danger zone." He says that once he gets a report that shows he is beginning to cross the line, he will begin to exercise and take control of his health. That's a recipe for disaster.

Don't even bother trying to balance anything else if your body is not in tune. All of your plans, ambitions, and goals are trivial if your engine is not tuned or dies. I'm not suggesting that you need to participate in triathlons. Simple, regular routines are all that is necessary. Discover or rediscover what it is you love to do to move your body and do it! Eliminating all exercise kills you a little more each day. As the outlaw Josey Wales once said "Get busy living or get busy dying." To which I'd only add, start out slow.

Before you do anything have your entire body checked out. Go to the various doctors (dentist, eye doctor, etc.) for a full physical and get a blueprint of your health. Get all the tests you need so you can have the complete picture, and be sure to select a primary physician to hold your records. In the event of an emergency, it is critical that your history be accessible.

Once you are cleared for physical activity, be proactive about your health and use the information from your doctors to devise a safe and effective physical routine that complements your overall condition. Find a routine you enjoy. It will take work, but if exercise is not a labor of love it will never become a part of who you are.

START WITH SOMETHING SIMPLE

As seductive as the ads can be, trust me on this one: buying the "Ab Maximizer-Cruncher Super-Quick Body-Fat Reducer machine" won't help. I can virtually guarantee it will only collect dust and end up selling at a fraction of its original price at your next garage sale. The reason they don't work is that because we pay good money for them, we tend to trick ourselves into expecting them to do the work for us. Don't allow yourself to get caught in this weird little mind game. Not to mention that most machines confine you to boring solo routines. I suggest starting with simple movements, such as taking a walk after dinner, light jogging (the pounding on your knees can be detrimental to the desired results, so be sure to look for a cushioned track or a dirt path), or a stretching routine. There are great stretching tapes at your local video store or online. You can always decide to add equipment later. I personally prefer activities that are inspirational, such as games that require strategy and a competitive spirit or outdoor activities that allow me to experience nature at the same time.

In addition, try to find opportunities for physical activity in your day-to-day routines, in case you can't get to your scheduled routine. For example, if given the choice between an elevator or escalator and the stairs, choose the stairs. Get off your train or bus one stop early and walk the rest of the way to work. If you work in an office and need to communicate with someone else in the office, walk to him or her instead of using the phone. Take a walk after lunch or dinner to help digestion and to get movement. Weeding your garden or mowing your grass also provides excellent physical exercise and mental meditation. Almost anything physical will do. Just find what works for you.

Pumping Iron

Strength training is another good choice with many benefits. As you add more muscle your body needs more calories just to maintain its weight. People who strength train for three months on a regular basis usually gain three pounds of muscle and have to eat 15 percent more calories to maintain their body weight. Someone who lifts weights for twenty-five minutes twice a week can lose up to nine pounds of fat and gain three pounds of muscle within two months. In addition, whereas aerobic activity burns calories only during the exercise, after strength training your body continues to burn calories for up to two hours. Let your muscles burn away those extra pounds while creating a sturdier frame. Strength training is not just for the young; it becomes more important as we age. Our bones become fragile, and the stronger our muscles are the better supported our structure will be. Again, only begin a strength routine once you have had a physical. Start slow and build up the routine with the growth in your muscle.

Mix It Up

Following the same routines usually makes us want to quit. It gets old, boring, stale. Keep alternating your activities so they are always fresh and invigorating. You'll notice that the following list of activities offers traditional and not-so-traditional suggestions for physical movement. As you'll see, exercise comes in many forms. It doesn't have to be intense to be productive, and you don't have to break a sweat (although sweating is good for you, it releases toxins from your body). Your body will respond to any level of movement. Just get going. And remember: consult with your doctor prior to starting any exercise program.

Physical Activities to Keep You in Motion

▶ Always be a kid #1: Go to a park and play on a swing with your kids or young relatives (do it with a kid or people will be suspicious of you).

▶ Always be a kid #2: Go for a run in the rain and splash through the puddles.

▶ Always be a kid #3: Chase, race, and run with the children in your life.

▶ Do any form of aerobic exercise—running, aerobic walking, swimming, jumping rope, rowing, and so on. Increasing your oxygen capacity through regular aerobic exercise burns calories and fat.

▶ Take a walk every night after dinner. It will help you to digest and reduces the urge to sit in front of the television and eat more. Make it a family ritual to discuss the day.

▶ Clean your house.

▶ Weed your garden.

▶ Mow your grass and rake your yard.

- Go dancing.

- Go swimming.

- Go bicycling on your own or join a cycling club.

- Take the stairs instead of elevators or escalators.

- Go mall walking. Walk the entire mall and be sure to look in almost all stores. (Resist the urge to buy.)

- Walk your dog. Run with him or her if you can.

- Take a yoga class.

- Take a martial arts class. It will contribute to your physical and mental discipline.

- Exercise in the cold. The body burns more calories in the cold by just keeping warm.

- Play Frisbee.

- Lift weights. Be sure to learn the proper method with a trainer.

- Jump rope.

- Do pushups and sit-ups.

Take a Break

Some people get caught up on the opposite end of the spectrum and use every waking minute to accomplish something. I sometimes get in this mode myself and have to catch myself and schedule some down time. If you're someone who's always running, I suggest you actively manage your rest. (You see, I told you there was a good part.) We have all read stories of young Japanese professionals dropping dead suddenly because of their relentless work schedules. Sure, those are extreme cases, but we should all heed the warning. As important as finding time to exercise is finding time to rest, whether sleeping, napping, or *just vegging on the couch.* I wrote that in italics to catch my mother's attention. She cannot bear to see my father sleep on the couch. Granted, he may be the president of this activity's fan club, but my point is that it is important for all of us to take regular timeouts.

Some studies show that we need seven, some say eight or even ten hours of sleep per night. I'm not here to back or refute any claim. Chances are you know how much rest your body needs in order to be productive and stay well. For instance, I know that when I don't regularly get eight hours of sleep I get run down and usually become susceptible to getting a cold. This is my signal to slow it down and get back on a regular resting schedule.

Take the time to refuel. It will promote healing, creativity, and inspiration, all of which drive our zest for life and keep our lives in balance.

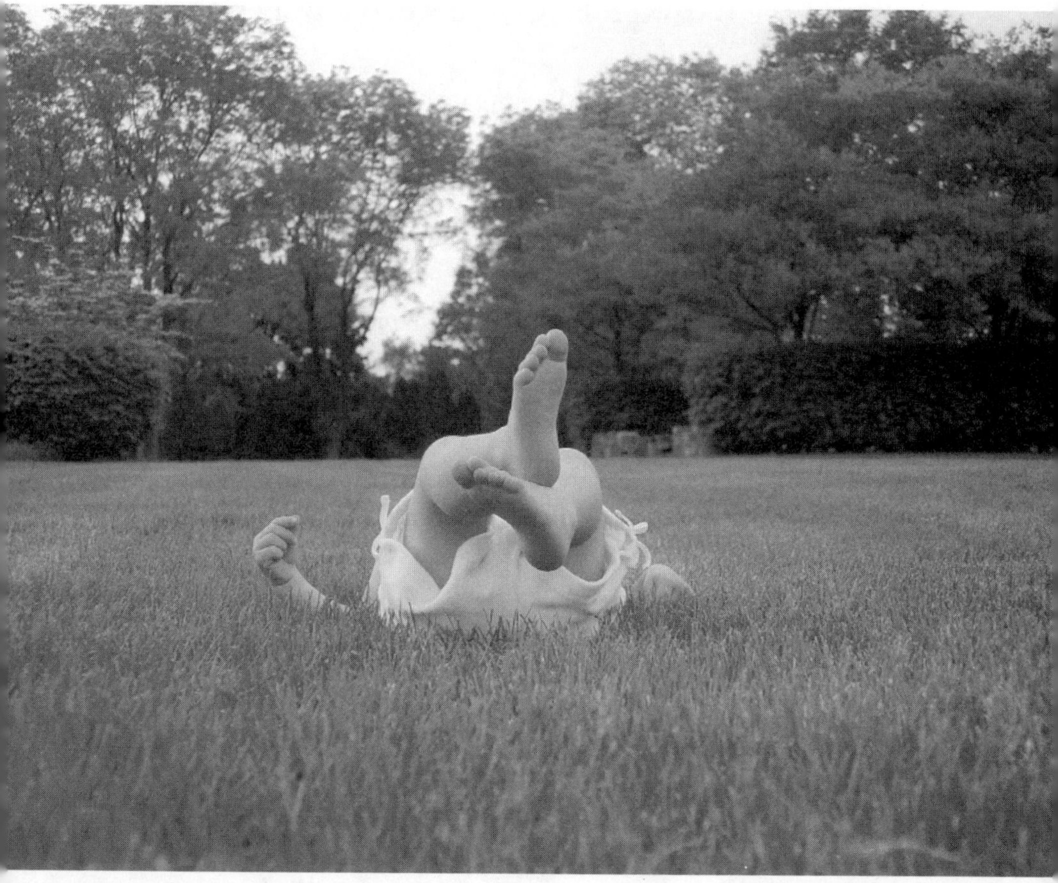

THE LIFE BALANCE PLAN FOR ACTIVE RELAXATION

▶ Take a nap in the middle of your day off. See what it's like to follow the natural rhythm of your body. A twenty- to thirty-minute rejuvenator is usually plenty. Don't let it go longer than one hour or you will risk falling into too deep a sleep and the invigorating intention of the nap will be lost.

▶ Meditate. This term can conjure up pictures of Indian yogis sitting in weird positions and chanting, but meditation is essentially focused relaxation. It is the practice of conscious, active relaxation exercises. A simple meditation involves focusing completely on your breathing. By just focusing on the in and out of your breath, you keep out the clutter that tries to filter back into your mind. Keep focusing on your breathing and you will eventually find that place where you can be at peace with yourself and your thoughts.

▶ Get a massage.

▶ Take a warm bath.

▶ Take a spa vacation, even if it's just for an afternoon.

All Work and No Play Makes . . .

All this talk of exercise and rest, but what about playtime? What's the point of living if you don't make time to enjoy yourself? We tend to worry about work and trivial issues with a great deal of tenacity; why not treat leisure time with the same gusto? Kids play whenever they can. If you think back, you probably stopped playing at the point where you had to think of ways to support yourself and perhaps a family so that you could eventually get rich and then get back to having fun. But somewhere along the line you got sidetracked and forgot the original goal. I would add that there's actually a major flaw in that plan in the first place. So many people work all their lives to retire and then become sick or die before they ever get to enjoy themselves. What a terrible shame.

Try to enjoy the journey, not just the destination. Fun is good for your health, too, but playtime is often the last thing on our list. That's why we have to *schedule it*. Having good playtime balances your drive to accomplish everything else in your life. Find those activities (and nonactivities) that let you escape the "real" world and allow yourself to get lost in them. Don't be surprised if these are the same things you do for intellectual or physical balance. That's true for lots of us.

Activities for Pleasure

I couldn't possibly list all the things you might want to do for pleasure. I'm sure you've got your own favorites, but here are a few ideas just to get the ball rolling:

▶ Go to or rent movies.

▶ Listen to music or go to concerts.

▶ Read books or magazines.

▶ Go fishing, kayaking, or canoeing.

▶ Cook.

▶ Take a long, leisurely walk with an old friend.

Parting Words

▶ Your body is your temple. Do everything in your power to keep it maintained.

▶ Remember to *schedule* activity and rest into your week. Set recurring appointments for exercise, play, and rest time.

▶ Make exercise, rest, and pleasure staple activities that will balance your physical being so you can achieve all your life goals.

▶ Know when to blow the whistle and end your day.

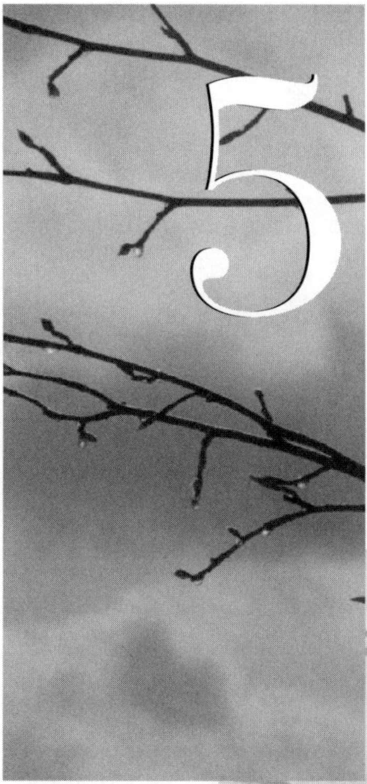

5 Spirituality Is in the Details

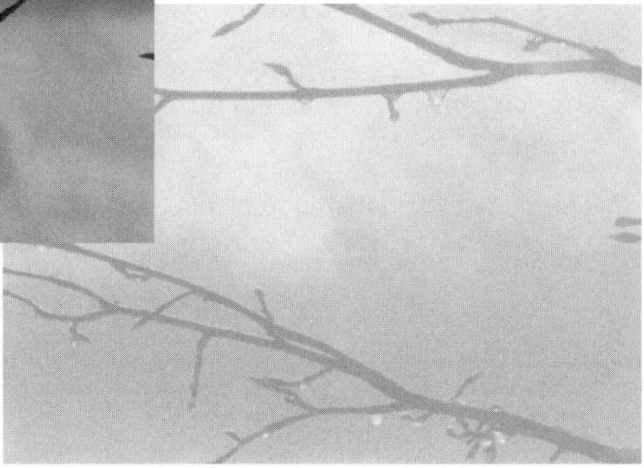

THE SPIRIT TEST

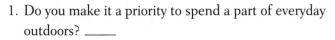

A. Never = 1 point
B. Sometimes = 2 points
C. Always = 3 points

1. Do you make it a priority to spend a part of everyday outdoors? _____

2. Do you think about your existence in relation to the rest of the natural world? _____

3. Do you make time to get out and explore nature? _____

4. Do you make time to disconnect from technology? _____

5. Are you conscious of reducing waste and pollution? _____

6. Do you go outside to be in the rain and snow? _____

7. Do you take time to appreciate a beautiful sunset or other natural scenes? _____

8. Are you considerate and mindful of animals and all natural creatures? _____

9. Do you grow and maintain plants, flowers, or vegetables? _____

10. Are you inspired by a beautiful day? _____

Scoring

Write your score next to each question number and then total.

1. _____

2. _____

3. _____

4. _____

5. _____

6. _____

7. _____

8. _____

9. _____

10. _____

Total: _____

Evaluation

10–15: It's time to reevaluate and take small steps to get on the path to achieving balance in this area.

16–20: You're on the path to balance in this pillar. Focus on your weak areas and you will take noticeable positive steps.

21–30: Congratulations! You're living at a high level of balance in this pillar. Determine the areas that will have the greatest impact on enhancing your life experiences.

Connecting with the Natural World

Will works in New York City but lives in a nearby suburb. He wakes up every day at 4 AM to go for a walk on a trail by his home. This escape feeds his desire to be connected with nature and gives him a physical energy boost that offsets his sedentary travel and confined workday.

Okay, perhaps Will's story seems extreme, but sometimes we have to look outside our routine or our comfort zone to find opportunities to experience the natural world, to feel connected. In *The Color Purple,* author Alice Walker wrote, "I think it pisses God off if you walk by the color Purple in a field somewhere and don't notice it." It doesn't take any particular religious conviction to see that the world is an incredible assembly of natural structures and events. The light reflected off the rising moon, the shifting colors of the sky, the sounds of breaking waves, the harmony in the animal kingdom, the grand elevation of mountains, and the clean freshness of the air we breathe are all wonders that have come together to create a natural balance in the world. But sometimes we forget to notice.

Perhaps you already wake up every day feeling connected to this great marvel of a creation, but many people just walk by without noticing. They're too wrapped up in life's details. But something is driving the rhythms within us and the world. The heightened sensitivity or responsiveness to that something is what I call spirituality—that desire to take your daily existence to a deeper level and really *experience* your connection to the mystery and majesty of life. My hope is that the practices we'll explore in this chapter will connect you to your own spiritual roots in nature and bring you into balance in this, the fourth of my six Pillars of Life Balance.

Be a Guide

I have a two-year-old daughter, Giana, whose arrival in my life has changed my perspective in so many ways. I often take her for walks and have made it my job to be her "World Guide." We look at every natural force in our little world. We go out in the rain and feel the drops land on our skin. We feel the grass under our bare feet and smell the flowers in our garden. When I look at her face and see the amazement as we discover something new, it drives home the fact that this is truly an amazing world we live in. Even if you don't have a young child, perhaps you have someone in your life to whom you could introduce the natural world. Experiencing nature through the eyes of a child, seeing things as if for the first time, is a delightful way to reconnect.

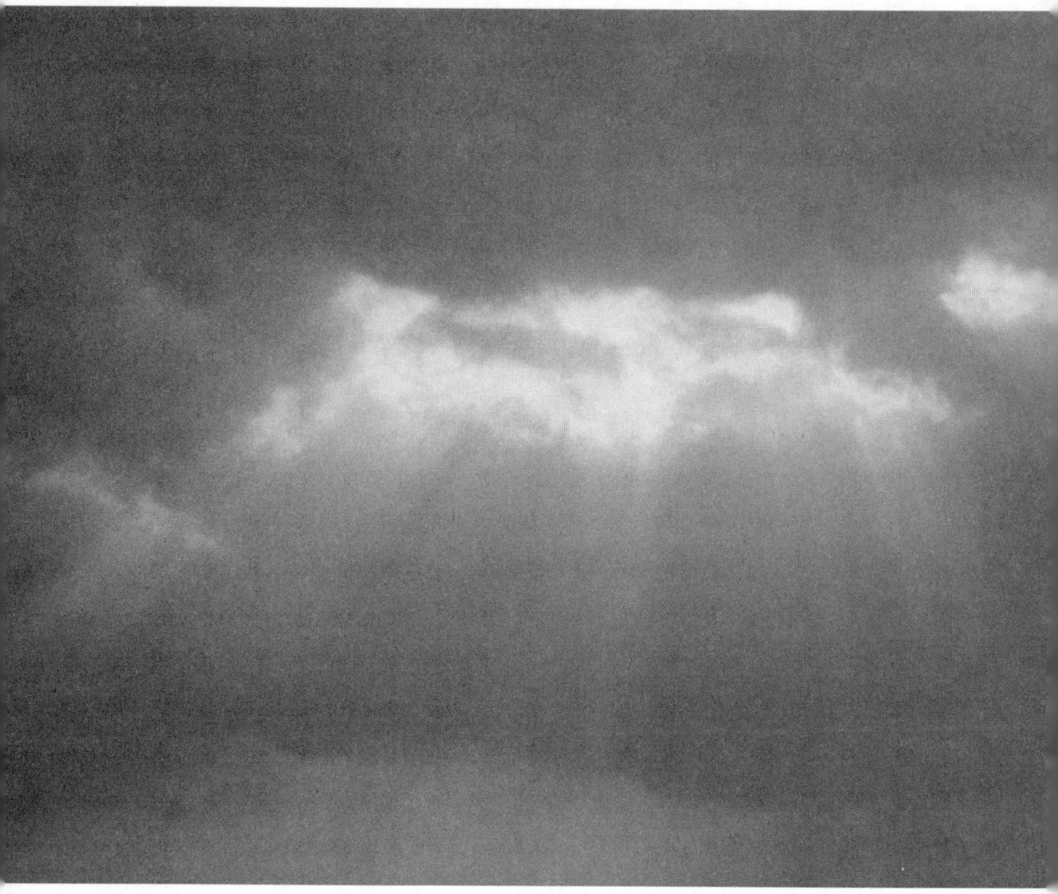

Get Out

Put on your boots, your shorts, your hat, whatever you need and get outside. Get away from the city and look for natural places with trees, grass, flowers, water, and unobstructed sunlight. Take a winter getaway or just a fall nature walk. Even if you're confined to a city, you undoubtedly have access to parks, zoos, botanical gardens, trails, and many other nature-inspired creations. There are no excuses to not experience some form of nature on a frequent basis to keep the bond alive that you share with the world. It's time to notice the details.

Try to spend part of every day doing nothing but being in your natural environment. Start with places that are close to your home so you can easily do this without much planning. Gradually look to expand your reach by experiencing natural places that you may have never considered. Whatever it takes, just be outside, watch what is going on around you, and practice awareness without any distractions. All of this will initiate or enhance your spiritual connection to the world.

As you stand looking at the natural world around you, think about what you are in relation to the larger picture. This will center you and calm your thinking. The world is an incredible place, and your commitment to achieving balance will be furthered by looking at life in the spiritual details.

20/20 Vision—

Activities That Inspire Spiritual Connections

▶ Walk in the rain in the forest, a park, or any quiet place. Feel the peace. Listen to the raindrops hitting the trees or the ground. Hear the natural rhythm it offers. Contrary to popular belief, you can't get sick by getting wet. If you have endured a shower you can walk in the rain.

▶ Take a moment to notice some detail about the natural world and realize how fortunate you are to be a part of it. Notice the visual beauty of the trees, listen to the sounds of the birds, smell the flowers.

▶ Just be. Pick a day and have no agenda except to just do nothing but hang around somewhere outside.

▶ Have a disconnected day. Unplug from all technology and media.

▶ Grow something. If you live in an apartment, grow an herb garden. Stay connected to the earth and the wonderful phenomenon of growing.

▶ Start a compost pile. Reduce the amount of garbage you produce by giving back to the earth.

▶ Experience the seasons. It is invigorating to go through them and feel the change and rejuvenation the earth goes through.

▶ Experience snow. Go snowshoeing, sledding, downhill or cross-country skiing, or just take a walk. There is peacefulness in the air during a snowfall; be a part of it.

▶ Have a listen. Listen to the birds, the wind, and the water. Enjoy the natural rhythm.

- ▶ Experience water. Go to a lake, the ocean, or any other natural body of water. You don't need to know how to swim; you can just stand in shallow areas and feel the sensation water gives to your body.

- ▶ Experience the visual art the world presents to us. Look at the dynamic shapes of the clouds, the radiant hues of the sun, the vivid color of flowers, the natural beauty and grace of birds, and the structural elegance of trees.

- ▶ Take a nature-inspired vacation. A bike, hike, kayak, or camping tour.

- ▶ Take a day to go to the zoo or, if you are daring, book a safari vacation.

- ▶ Wake up early and watch the sun rise. Watch it set as well.

- ▶ Take a trip to a natural wonder. The Grand Canyon, the rain forest, Joshua Tree. Look for tour operators to suggest others.

- ▶ Have a picnic. There is a peaceful aura surrounding this experience.

- ▶ Go to an outdoor concert at a park. You will experience a natural energy from the combination of the two.

- ▶ Become a nature photographer. Use any type of camera and begin to build an album of your favorite natural images.

- ▶ Go apple and pumpkin picking or any other similar activity.

- ▶ Join a wildlife or nature club. They provide well-guided and structured trips to keep you connected.

Parting Words

▶ Do something each day just because it nourishes your spirit.

▶ Make a commitment to yourself to spend a part of every day in nature.

▶ Schedule it. Take the morning or the end of the day, but be sure to put a spiritual connection time on your schedule. Leave yourself enough time for decompressing from the busy world around you. Use the time for reflection and centering.

6 The Right Fuel

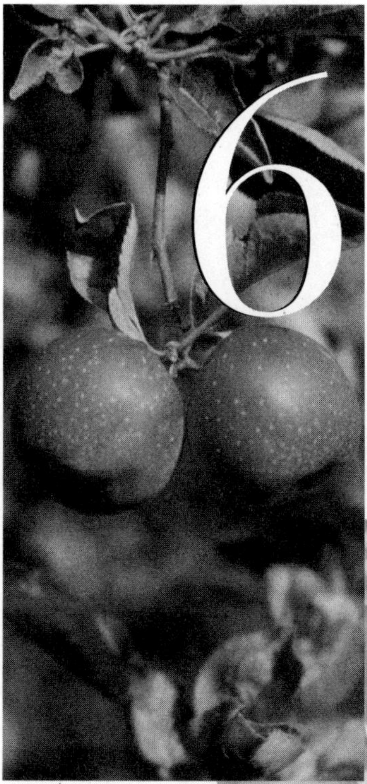

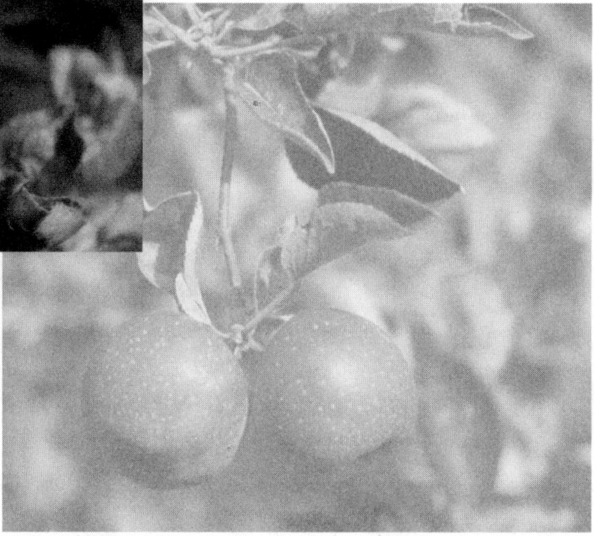

The Fuel Test

A. Never = 1 point
B. Sometimes = 2 points
C. Always = 3 points

1. Do you educate yourself in the principles of proper nutrition? _____

2. Do you go to a health professional and develop a blueprint for your nutritional needs? _____

3. Do you follow a balanced diet? _____

4. Do you read the labels before buying or eating food products? _____

5. Do you ask for ingredients at restaurants? _____

6. Do you avoid fast, junk, and processed foods? _____

7. Do you buy fresh fruits and vegetables? _____

8. Do you avoid sugar? _____

9. Do you shop for healthy foods in a grocery or health food store? _____

10. Do you believe that eating affects your overall mood and outlook? _____

Scoring

Write your score next to each question number and then total.

1. _____
2. _____
3. _____
4. _____
5. _____
6. _____
7. _____
8. _____
9. _____
10. _____

Total:_____

Evaluation

10–15: It's time to reevaluate and take small steps to get on the path to achieving balance in this area.

16–20: You're on the path to balance in this pillar. Focus on your weak areas and you will take noticeable positive steps.

21–30: Congratulations! You're living at a high level of balance in this pillar. Determine the areas that will have the greatest impact on enhancing your life experiences

Get on the Right Train

Joe was thirty-two and had just had his first son. He was not overweight but had a very unhealthy eating style. He drank large amounts of soda and ate donuts and greasy fast food. He looked fine, could play sports when he wanted to, and had no reason to change his eating routine. Suddenly his ankles became swollen and painful. A trip to the doctor revealed that his kidneys had shut down. He was prescribed steroids, and his condition eventually subsided. His doctors pointed to his diet and said he needed to make changes. Joe felt the first signs of mortality. While he was in the hospital he wondered if he would ever take his son to a ball game. He immediately committed to change.

Many people go through life with an unhealthy diet and are lucky enough to not have any problems or conditions. They preach, "Look at me, I eat anything I want and I'm fine." This is true for smokers and drinkers as well. We have all heard a story about someone's eighty-five-year-old grandfather who eats anything, drinks alcohol, and smokes. But not only are these people exceptions, longevity doesn't always equate with health. Just look at the skin hues of a long-time smoker or drinker. Not exactly a glowing endorsement for abusing your body.

We've all heard the statistics about obesity. Americans, including children, have higher rates of obesity now than at any time in our history. If you eat a diet high in fats, particularly saturated fats, and you simultaneously are not exercising to burn off the fat, the body will produce fat cells. Once your body makes a fat cell, it will never lose it. Your cells may shrink as you lose weight, but those fat cells will never disappear, which explains people's tendency toward obesity. The more fat cells you have the more body fat you will have.

Fat cells multiply rapidly during a person's teen years, so if you are a parent, do whatever you can to reduce your children's intake of fat and sugar and help them develop healthy eating habits. The younger these habits are developed, the more likely they will stick for a lifetime.

And let's not get too hung up on the scale either. Plenty of thin people are unhealthy eaters, too. You may look good on the outside but your inner core may be deteriorating. Over time, not eating properly *will* come back to haunt you, no matter how good you look today.

Everything you eat and drink has an effect on your body's health, your mood, ambition, and self-image. They are the fuel you use to run your engine. Many of us have traded off quality for convenience. In fact Americans eat more chemically treated food, pesticides, fatty oils, and preservatives than any other culture. This just means it's more challenging to find ways to eat healthy and overcome the pressure to follow the majority. But you've simply got to do it. Getting the right fuel is absolutely critical to a body in balance.

I remember the day I committed to changing the way I eat. I was twenty years old and I was finishing a typical dinner with my family. It was a hot summer night, and we had just had steak, frozen onion rings, and rice. I stood up from the table and felt so bloated and greasy that I proclaimed that from this day on I would take control of my eating habits and develop a healthy menu and lifestyle for myself. Believe it or not, I never looked back. I took a nutrition course to get the basics and started reading health magazines for additional concepts and balanced meal suggestions. I started out by cutting just red meat and continuing to eat chicken and fish and then gradually became a vegetarian. I'm not advocating that all my readers become vegetarian, just that you become proactive about what you eat.

Let's start with the basics—portion control. Just because everything these days is available in super-jumbo-colossal-grande size doesn't mean we should consume larger and larger quantities of everything. In fact, you don't need to feel full after every meal. You can, over a relatively short period of time, begin to feel satisfied with eating less. I recommend eating several small meals throughout the day rather than the typical three large meals. With smaller meals eaten closer

together your body can absorb nutrients more efficiently and your energy level will remain steady as a result. It's important not to skip meals, too. This will help avoid bingeing and hoarding. You are training your body to eat differently, and it can take time and a lot of discipline to adjust. But aren't you worth it? Of course, *what* you eat is most important of all.

Make your food choices a priority in the same way you would choose a doctor, a car, or a job. Weigh the pluses and minuses of the things you eat and look at the effects they will have on your body. Pay attention to the fine print.

Remember, too, that your eating habits affect your overall demeanor, not just your waistline. Eating disorders are related to emotional and psychological issues and need to be treated with professional help, but there are less severe habits that many of us fall into from time to time also based on our emotional state. Making deliberate unhealthy choices and bingeing can be manifestations of a lack of balance in other areas.

I urge you to establish personal eating rules and parameters that you will not allow yourself to deviate from. Having this regimented approach to eating will build a strong foundation that will empower you to resist temptation and not allow yourself to be affected by outside forces. Easy? Not at all. It takes tremendous willpower and commitment to change the way you eat, but the payoff is beyond measure. Do you have to be perfect? Of course not. No one is. I go out to dinner and have take-out pizza every now and then. But a disciplined eating routine is a foundation for discipline in all other areas of your life. Harsh, perhaps, but without discipline, there is no balance.

The Life Balance Plan for Getting the Right Fuel

Before deciding to change your diet, see a doctor and get a full physical. This is a must for anyone seeking balance in their life. Unless you are properly informed about your overall physical condition you cannot make intelligent choices. Also note that no cookbook, diet, or nutrition plan is appropriate for everyone. The menus and concepts I will suggest here are the ones I use in my life. They have proven effective in my overall health, and they are adaptable to almost everyone. We'll be looking at the following four elements:

Quality

Quantity

Diversity

Consistency

QUALITY

Unfortunately, the quality of the food supply in this country is in decline. But we have the power to change that. If we shifted our focus and put food at the top of our daily priority list, we would demand high-quality products, and the food industry would have to comply. No matter what health program you follow, there are some general dos and don'ts. These are the ones that make the most sense to me. I put the don'ts first because elimination will have the most immediate and positive effect on your body.

Don'ts

▶ No artificial, processed, or refined ingredients. These are found mostly in poor-quality snack foods.

▶ Reduce your saturated fat intake. Avoid fried foods, fatty meats, and dessert foods that contain partially hydrogenated vegetable oils.

▶ Reduce the wrong carbohydrates. Breads and pastas made with white flour, as well as the refined sugars found in most dessert items, are the wrong carbohydrates.

▶ Eat less high-fat dairy products, namely butter and cheese.

▶ Reduce your salt intake.

▶ Eliminate excessive refined sugar.

▶ Reduce or eliminate alcohol.

▶ Beware fat-free foods. Many manufacturers boast fat free but then add high amounts of sugar to provide a rich, sweet taste. The result may be fat free but extremely high in calories.

▶ Reduce the use of heavy sauces, creams, and salad dressings. Always ask for the sauce on the side and use sparingly for flavor.

▶ Reduce or eliminate soda as your primary drink.

▶ Cut down on greasy packaged snacks: cakes, cookies, chips, and pretzels.

Dos

▶ Shop for natural and whole foods. A high-quality grocery store or a health food grocery store is your best bet for finding whole grains and quality produce.

▶ Make sure most of your meals are high in protein, vegetables, and fruit. High-protein foods include fish (just be careful to buy and eat fish that are farmed without antibiotics or hormones or caught in a way that supports a healthy environment—see *www.mbayaq.org/cr/seafoodwatch.asp*, the Monterey Bay Aquarium's Seafood Watch Program Web site, for more information), eggs, low-fat cottage cheese, poultry, lean red meat, tofu, tempeh, and quinoa.

▶ Eat food that is baked, broiled, or grilled.

▶ Eat leaner meats. Chicken should always be skinless, and look for varieties that are not treated with hormones or antibiotics.

▶ Eat the "good carbohydrates"—beans, whole grains, squash, sweet potatoes, fruit, and quinoa (yes, it's both a protein and a "complex" carbohydrate).

▶ Eat more fruits and vegetables. Be sure to eat five to eight servings of fruits and vegetables a day in a large variety and different colors. They are low in calories and fat and are filling because they have fiber.

▶ Eat the "good" fats: olive oil, walnuts (which are also high in fiber), and peanut butter (be sure you don't have an allergy to nuts; some nut allergies can be fatal).

▶ Eat foods high in Omega 3 fatty acids: salmon and tuna, baked, broiled, or grilled; walnuts; and ground flaxseed or flaxseed oil.

▶ Eat high-fiber foods: raspberries and beans, in particular.

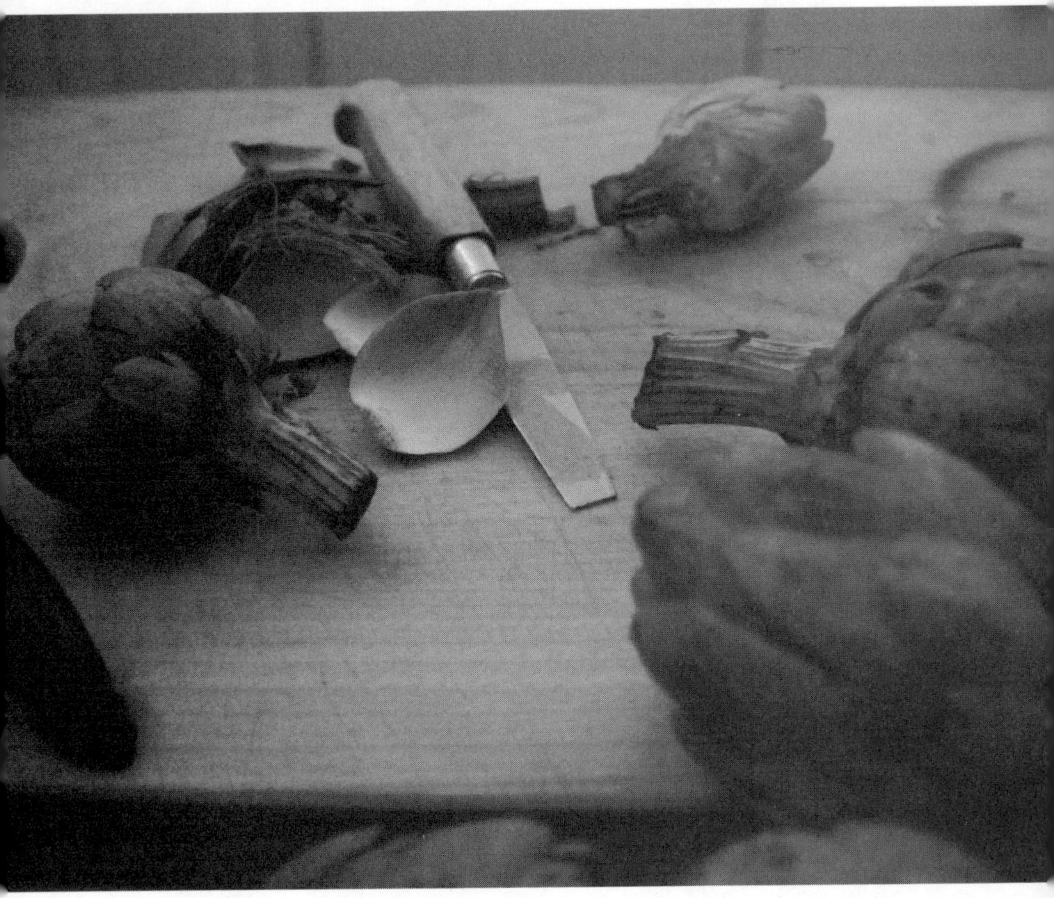

- ▶ Ask waiters in restaurants for ingredients and preparation methods —don't be afraid to ask to eliminate certain ingredients, reduce salt, and alter portions.

- ▶ Eat garlic, lots and lots of garlic.

- ▶ Eat egg whites, but not the yolks.

- ▶ Eat soy products: soymilk, tofu, veggie burgers.

- ▶ Drink fresh juices and large amounts of water.

- ▶ Eat healthy snacks: popcorn (no butter and reduced salt), raisins, rice cakes, and nuts.

QUANTITY

This one's simple. Practice control of portion size by eating six small meals throughout the day (you'll find a sample plan on p. 110–11).

DIVERSITY

Vary food groups, ingredients, and preparation to ensure nutrition and cut down on boredom.

CONSISTENCY

Eat on a schedule. This will enable the body to self-regulate your hunger patterns and create a healthy rhythm to eating.

TIME MANAGEMENT

Break your eating day into six meals and schedule them. Set a reminder on your organizer. Avoid skipping any of the meals to prevent feeling famished and trigger overeating.

Where should you start? The most important way to approach change is gradually. Do not shock your body into drastic changes—the results will be temporary. Remember, this is not a short-term trip; this will be your lifelong journey, so you must treat it as a major life adjustment. Start with one meal a day at the beginning and then gradually shift your entire diet.

20/20 Vision

THE LIFE BALANCE DAILY EATING SCHEDULE

A few words about fluids before we start: Drinking lots of water and/or fruit juice (without added sugar) throughout the day will keep you hydrated and can ease feelings of hunger.

1. The Jump Start.
This is what I call your first meal of the day. It will set the tone for your energy level. Avoid excessive sugar, fats, and carbohydrates. Try scrambled egg whites, five-minute oatmeal, or whole-grain cereal.

2. The Energizer I.
You will burn off most of the Jump Start meal just by getting your day started. That's why you will need a late-morning snack to boost your energy level as the morning meal wears off. A piece of fruit or a smoothie is an ideal late-morning Energizer I.

3. The Mid-Day Refuel.
Here's where I differ with many other diet planners. I say don't eat a big lunch. The body's natural rhythm is toward a tendency to rest around midday. You don't want to contribute to a feeling of sluggishness by eating a big meal, which takes extra energy to digest. Try a chickpea, lettuce, and tomato salad, a vegetable wrap, a veggie burger without the bun or a rice salad.

4. The Energizer II.

This is an afternoon snack to help bridge your energy level from lunch to dinner. If you wait until dinner you will most likely be famished and will overeat to compensate for the depleted energy. Try rice cakes, fruit, popcorn (no butter or salt), or a smoothie drink.

5. The Late-Day Refuel.

Otherwise known as dinner. Break the traditional mold and avoid a big meal that leaves you stuffed. Load up on the vegetables and proteins and reduce the amount of breads and pastas.

6. The Wind-Down.

Have one more small snack or a cup of tea to end the day. Best not to eat within an hour of bedtime.

20/20 VISION —

THE LIFE BALANCE PLAN
FOR *Organizing* THE WAY YOU APPROACH EATING

▶ Reduce your consumption of take-out food and try to prepare your own meals.

▶ Ask waiters in restaurants to name the ingredients and preparation methods—don't be afraid to ask to eliminate certain ingredients, reduce salt, and alter preparations.

▶ When traveling, take your own food on airplane trips and seek out simple, healthy meals in hotels and restaurants. Fruit and vegetables should be your staples while traveling.

▶ Plan your meals for the week by writing up a daily menu. Think about what you would like to eat (see recipes below). Pick up a healthy cookbook and plan meals from it. Do a full week. This will cut down on the anxiety of deciding what to eat from meal to meal and eliminate the last-minute choice to just get take-out.

▶ Make a list *before* you go shopping. By having specific meals in mind you will avoid overbuying and the practice of stocking up on unnecessary items that will tempt you to eat them. Many people buy too much food and eat it all because otherwise "it will go bad."

▶ Choose your markets carefully. Clean and fresh are the keys.

▶ Pay attention to details. Look carefully at ingredients, expiration dates, and freshness.

▶ Do it yourself. If you take the time to prepare your own meals, you will save money and control the quality. I know, I know, you have no time, but again, what is more important? I use Sunday night as my food preparation time. Here are some ways to prepare your meals for the week. (Also see recipes below.)

○ Breakfast: You can make a hot breakfast two or three times a week. In addition, cereals, five-minute oatmeal, and fruit are easily prepared and need little prep time.

○ Snacks: smoothies, fruit, low-fat granola bars, raisins, rice cakes, popcorn, and yogurt are simple low- or no-prep snacks.

○ Lunch: make meals that you can put in a resealable bag or plastic container and use them up every day. Most salads and sandwiches can be made ahead of time and will last a week.

○ Dinner: try to cook a fresh meal at least twice a week. In addition, make meals ahead of time and freeze them for convenience.

▶ Keep a food journal. Keep track of what, when, and how much you eat at each meal and your mood at the time you ate. You will begin to see patterns that may help you alter your eating habits.

▶ So, you're never going to cook or prepare your own meals and you're surrounded by McDonalds, Burger King, Subway, Taco Bell, and Wendy's. What can you do?

○ Go for the salads first.

○ Always choose grilled instead of fried.

○ Choose white-meat chicken over burgers.

○ Skip the sauces and dressings or ask for them on the side.

○ Don't order jumbo anything.

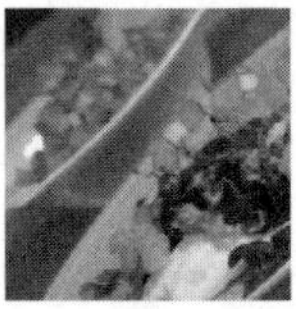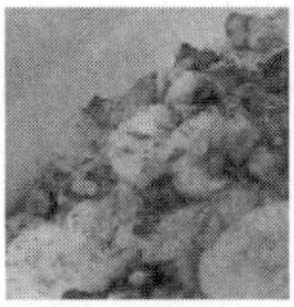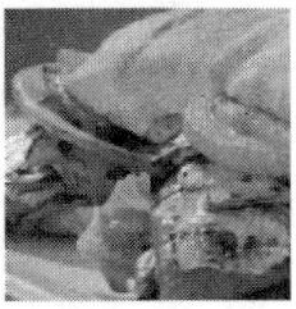

20/20 Vision—

My Life Balance Mini-Cookbook of Healthy Recipes

Try these recipes to help jump-start a proper nutrition program:

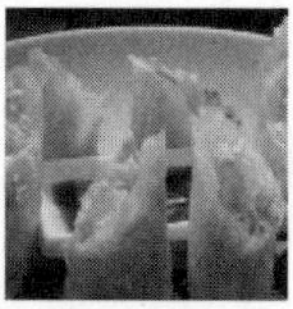
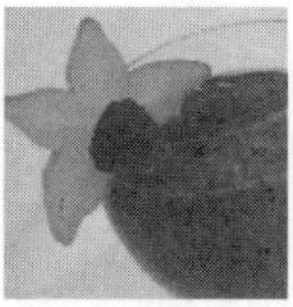
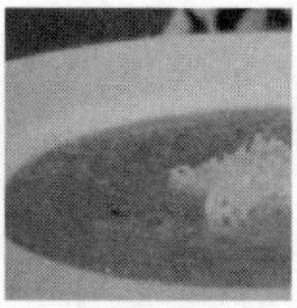
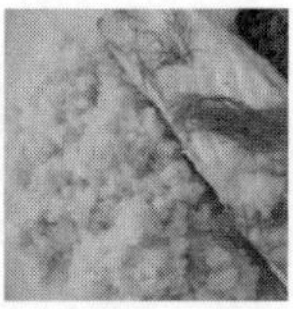
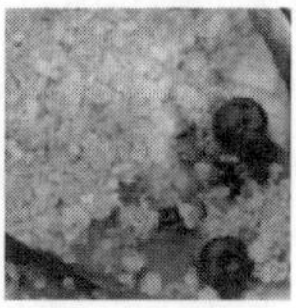

Black and White Omelet
with Fresh Tomato Salsa

SALSA

4 ripe tomatoes, finely chopped
2 tablespoons red onion, finely chopped
½ clove finely minced garlic
½ teaspoon jalapeno pepper, finely minced
1 teaspoon chopped cilantro
sea salt

In a medium bowl mix together all ingredients. Salt to taste. Set aside.
Let stand for at least one half hour.

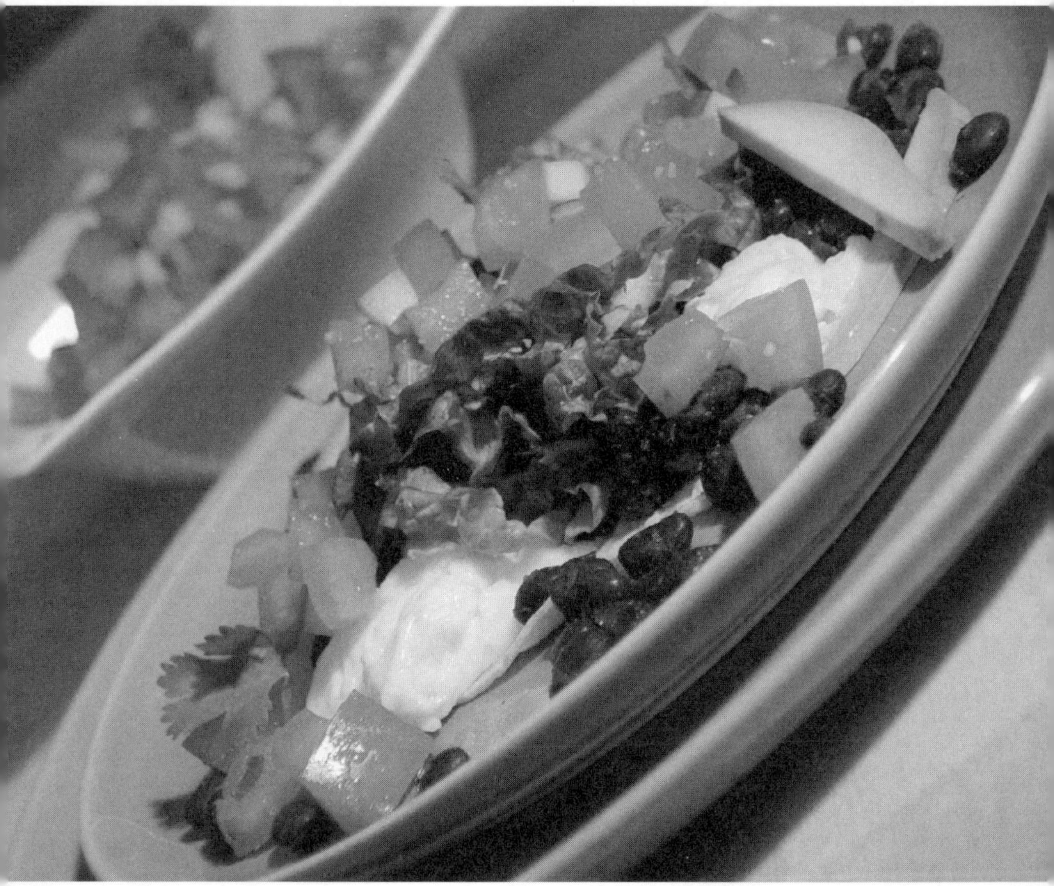

Black and White Omelet

⅔ cup canned black beans, rinsed and drained
⅛ teaspoon ground cumin
⅛ teaspoon garlic powder
⅛ teaspoon chili powder
cayenne pepper and sea salt to taste
½ teaspoon extra virgin olive oil
6 egg whites
2 corn tortillas
1 cup shredded lettuce
½ sliced avocado

Preheat oven to 325°.

In a medium bowl, sprinkle the rinsed black beans with the ground cumin, garlic powder, chili powder, cayenne pepper, and sea salt. Mix together. Microwave three to four minutes or use a covered saucepan and heat until warm.

Wrap corn tortillas in foil and place in oven for five minutes. Remove and set aside.

In a medium bowl, separate the egg whites. Place a large skillet on medium heat. Once the pan is hot pour in the olive oil; wait fifteen seconds and then add egg whites. Cook until fluffy. Season with salt.

Arrange warm corn tortillas on plates and top each with the egg whites, warm black beans, shredded lettuce, and sliced avocado. Spoon fresh tomato salsa on top and serve. Serves two.

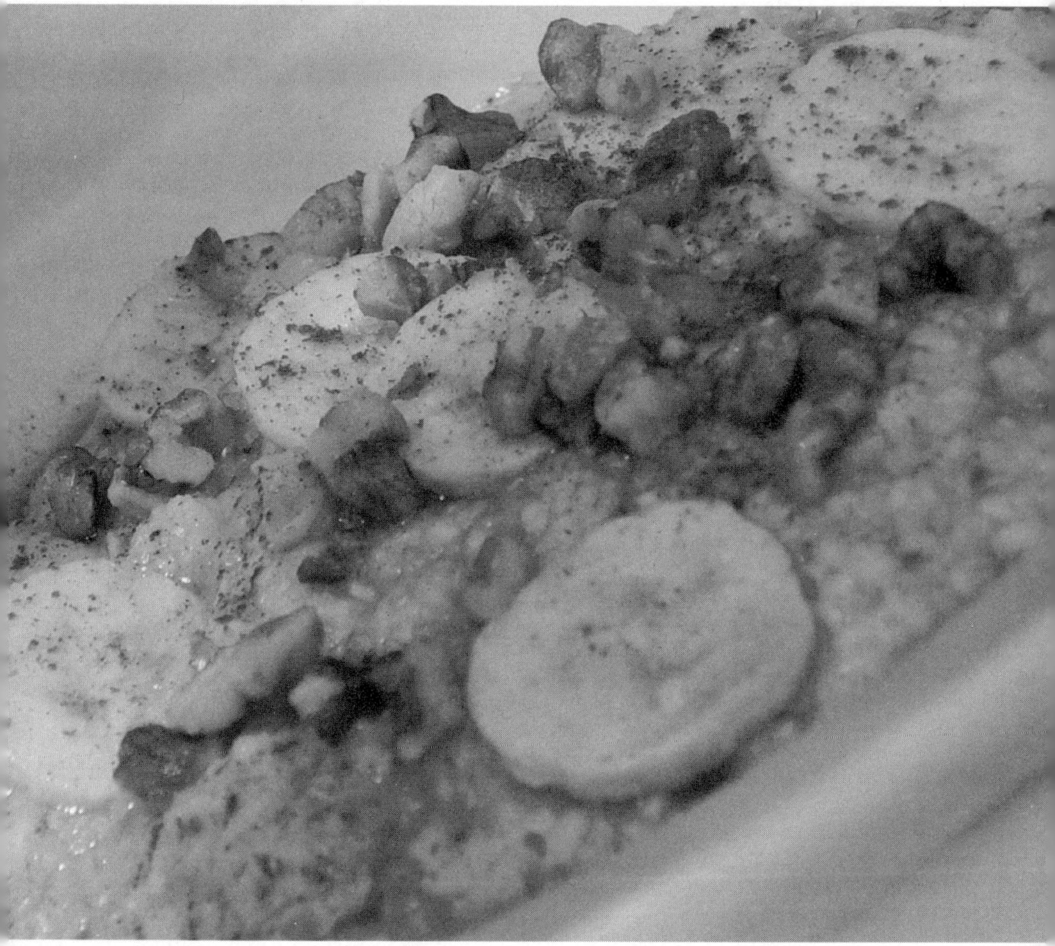

Banana Maple Walnut Oatmeal

1 cup quick-cook dry oatmeal
1 ripe banana, sliced thin
2 tablespoons chopped toasted walnuts
1 tablespoon pure maple syrup
ground cinnamon

Prepare oats according to directions. Divide cooked oats into two bowls. Top each bowl with the sliced banana and toasted walnuts. Drizzle with pure maple syrup and sprinkle with ground cinnamon. Serve warm. Serves two.

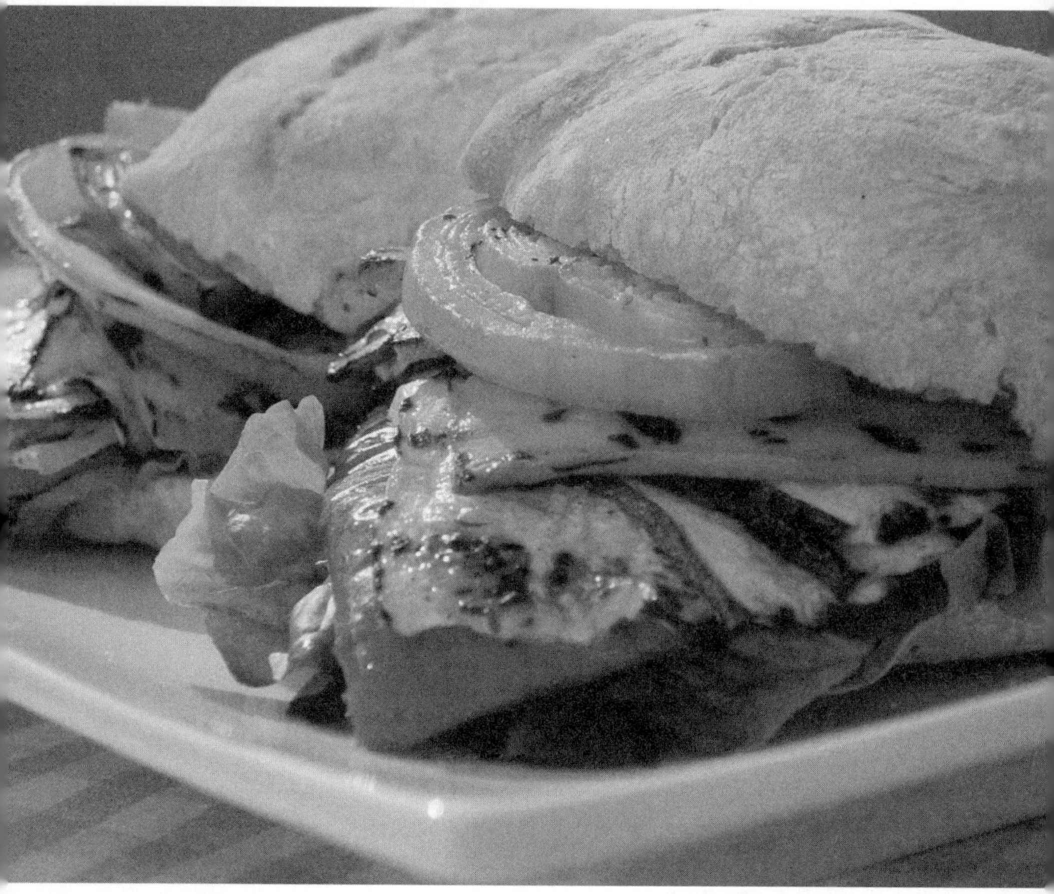

Grilled Vegetable Sandwich with White Bean Hummus

HUMMUS

15-ounce can of cannelloni beans, rinsed and drained
2 tablespoons extra virgin olive oil
½ garlic clove
¼ teaspoon dry ground oregano
¼ cup of water
sea salt and fresh ground pepper

In a blender puree the cannelloni beans, olive oil, garlic clove, ground oregano, and half of the water to a smooth, spreadable consistency, using more water to thin if necessary. Season with salt and fresh ground pepper. Set aside. You will have plenty left over for a great dip for raw vegetables.

Marinade

½ garlic clove, minced
1 tablespoon fresh lemon juice
2 tablespoons extra virgin olive oil
sea salt and fresh ground pepper to taste

Grilled Vegetables

1 zucchini, sliced thin lengthwise
1 yellow squash, sliced thin lengthwise
1 red bell pepper cut in half with seeds and stems removed
½ red onion, sliced thin
2 carrots, sliced thin lengthwise
lettuce

Prepare marinade in a large bowl, starting with fresh lemon juice and minced garlic. Whisk in extra virgin olive oil. Season with salt and fresh ground pepper. Set aside.

Grill the vegetables until char marks appear. After they are cooked, toss them in the marinade. Bring vegetables to room temperature.

Assemble sandwich by spreading a generous amount of white bean hummus on both sides of the bread, preferably a rustic, whole-grain bread, sliced horizontally. Layer on lettuce and grilled vegetables. Slice and serve. Serves two.

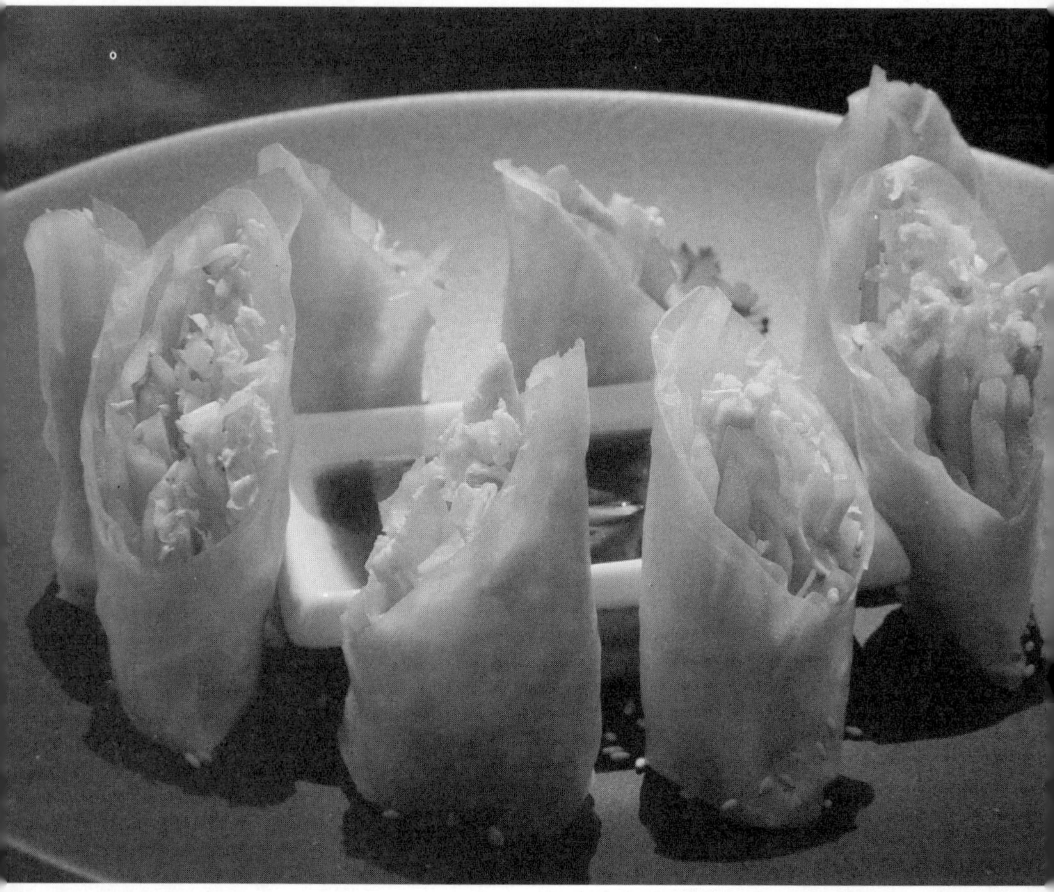

Spring Rolls and Dipping Sauce

GINGER SOY SESAME DIPPING SAUCE

½ cup soy sauce
2 tablespoons rice wine vinegar
1 tablespoon toasted sesame oil
½ teaspoon fresh ginger, finely minced

SPRING ROLLS

1 package of spring roll wrappers, approximately 20
4 ounces tempeh
½ napa cabbage, shredded
2 carrots, shredded
1 red bell pepper, sliced into fine julienne
3 green onions, sliced lengthwise
2 tablespoons toasted sesame seeds

In a medium bowl, combine the soy sauce, rice wine vinegar, toasted sesame oil, and fresh ginger. Remove half of sauce for dipping.

To create the spring roll filling, slice tempeh into matchstick-size julienne. Place into medium bowl with leftover sauce. Toss, let stand for five minutes. Add napa cabbage, carrots, red bell pepper, and green onions, making sure to coat vegetables with sauce. Add toasted sesame seeds.

Prepare spring roll wrappers by soaking them individually in cold water for ten seconds or until pliable. Place on work surface and add the filling into the wrappers. Roll up halfway and fold in sides, then roll rest of the way. Serve with dipping sauce. Serves four.

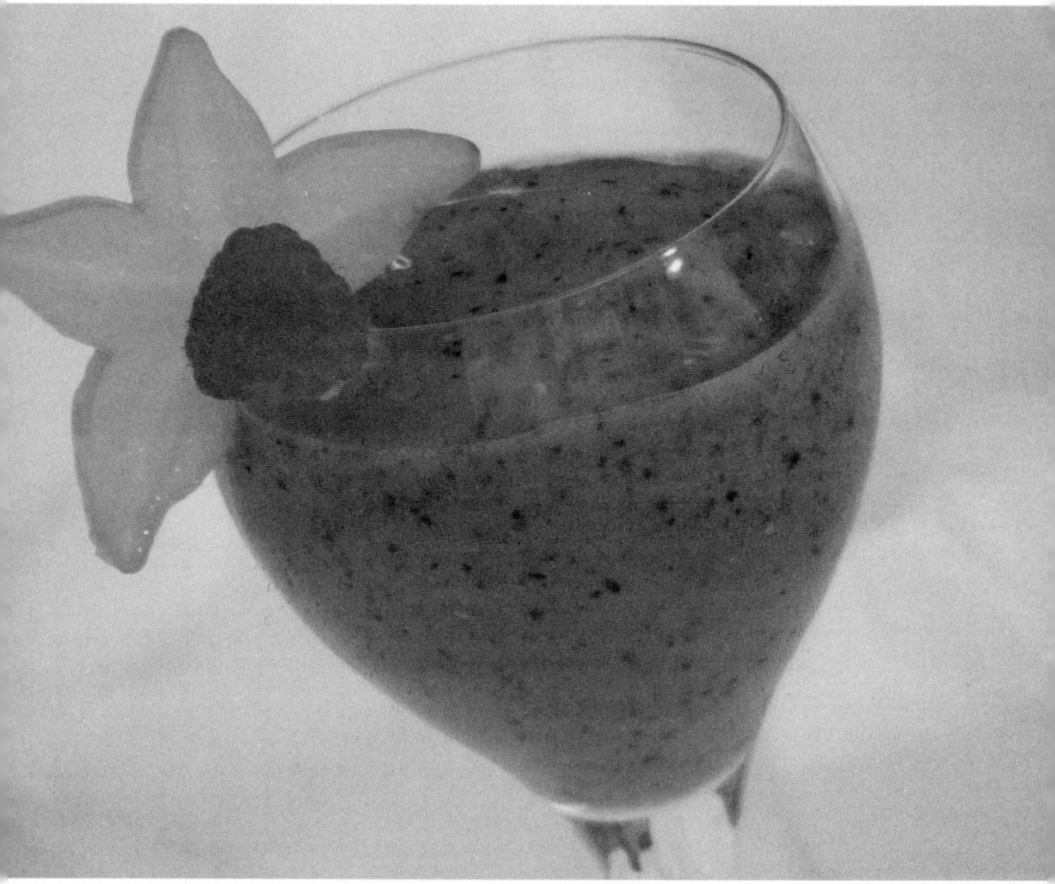

Fresh Fruit Smoothies

½ cup frozen peeled ripe banana*
2 frozen strawberries*
¼ cup frozen blueberries*
⅛ cup fresh pineapple
⅛ cup fresh mango
2 cups fresh orange, apple, or other fruit juice

*freeze ahead of time

In a blender, puree all ingredients, thinning to slushy consistency with fresh juice. Serve chilled in a glass. Serves two.

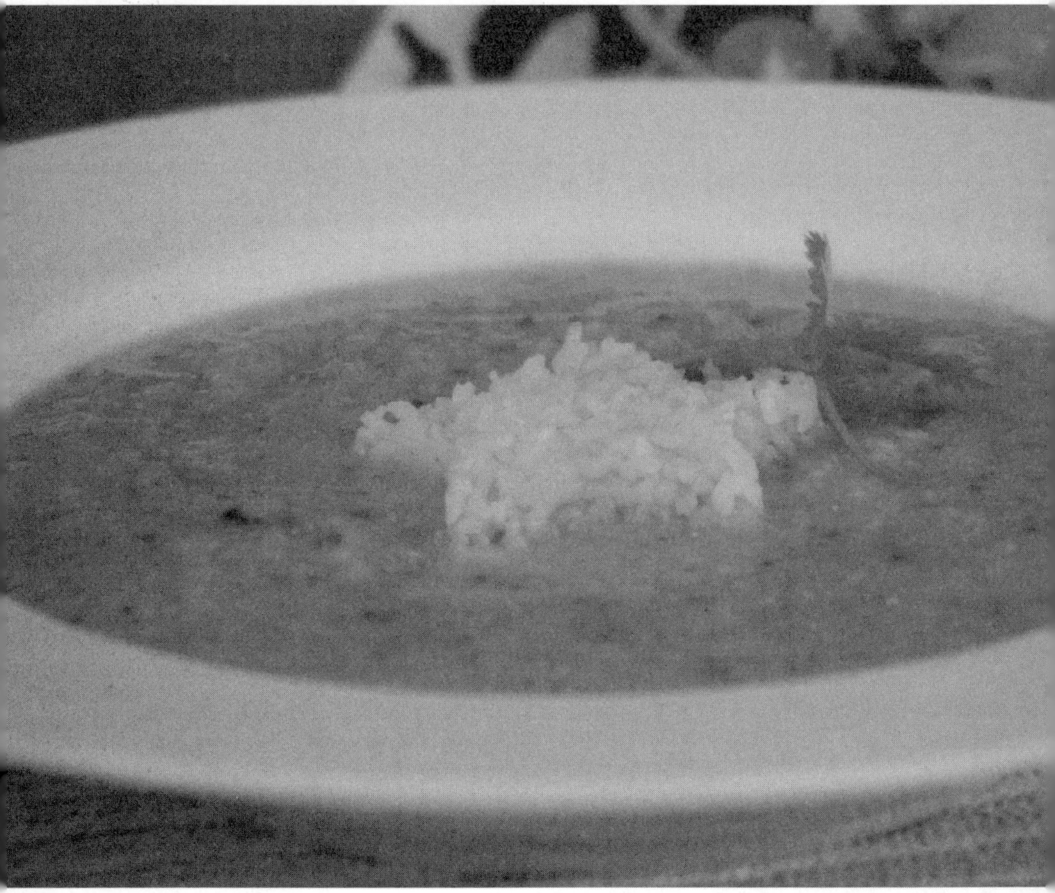

Red Lentil Soup with Brown Rice

3 tablespoons extra virgin olive oil
1 teaspoon cumin seed
1 teaspoon mustard seed
1 teaspoon turmeric
2 garlic cloves, chopped
1 medium onion, diced
3 celery stalks, chopped
2 carrot sticks, chopped
2 tomatoes, diced
2 cups dry red lentils
¼ cup shelled sunflower seeds (optional)
5½ cups of water
¼ cup fresh cilantro
sea salt

Heat the olive oil in a large stockpot. Add cumin seed, mustard seed, turmeric, garlic cloves, and onion. Cook until seeds start to pop and onion is translucent. Add celery, carrots, and tomatoes. Cook for five minutes. Add red lentils and sunflower seeds. Cook for three minutes. Add water and bring up to a simmer stirring periodically. Once simmering, turn down heat. Add cilantro and cook soup until lentils and vegetables are soft (approximately half an hour). Puree small batches in blender. Season to taste. Serve with brown rice (cook according to package directions). This is a perfect soup to freeze. Serves four.

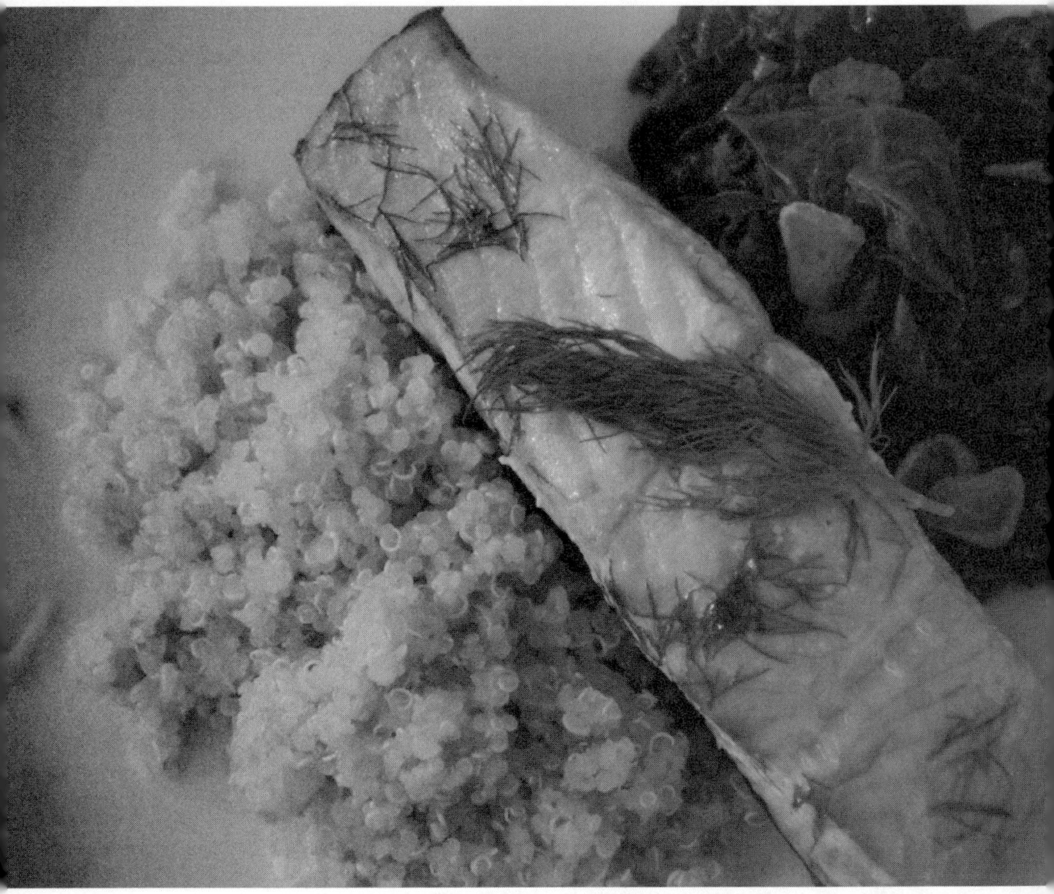

Roasted Salmon over Quinoa and Baby Spinach

2 salmon fillets, 4–5 ounces each
2 tablespoons fresh lemon juice
4 tablespoons extra virgin olive oil
1 sprig of fresh dill, torn into pieces
fresh ground pepper
½ cup dry quinoa
1 garlic clove, crushed
1 tablespoon soy sauce
1 bunch fresh baby spinach, cleaned thoroughly
2 tablespoons extra virgin olive oil
1 garlic clove, sliced
sea salt and fresh ground pepper

Preheat oven to 450°. In a medium-size bowl, whisk together fresh lemon juice, extra virgin olive oil, fresh dill, and fresh ground pepper. Rinse and dry salmon. Place into marinade. Refrigerate for fifteen minutes.

Prepare quinoa according to package directions, adding crushed garlic clove and soy sauce in place of salt.

Remove salmon from marinade and place on roasting rack, skin side down. Roast in oven for approximately eight minutes or until cooked through and the flesh begins to flake.

In a sauté pan, heat extra virgin olive oil on medium heat. Add sliced garlic. Cook until golden. Add baby spinach, turning until wilted. Season with salt and fresh ground pepper. Arrange quinoa, salmon, and baby spinach on plate and serve. Serves two.

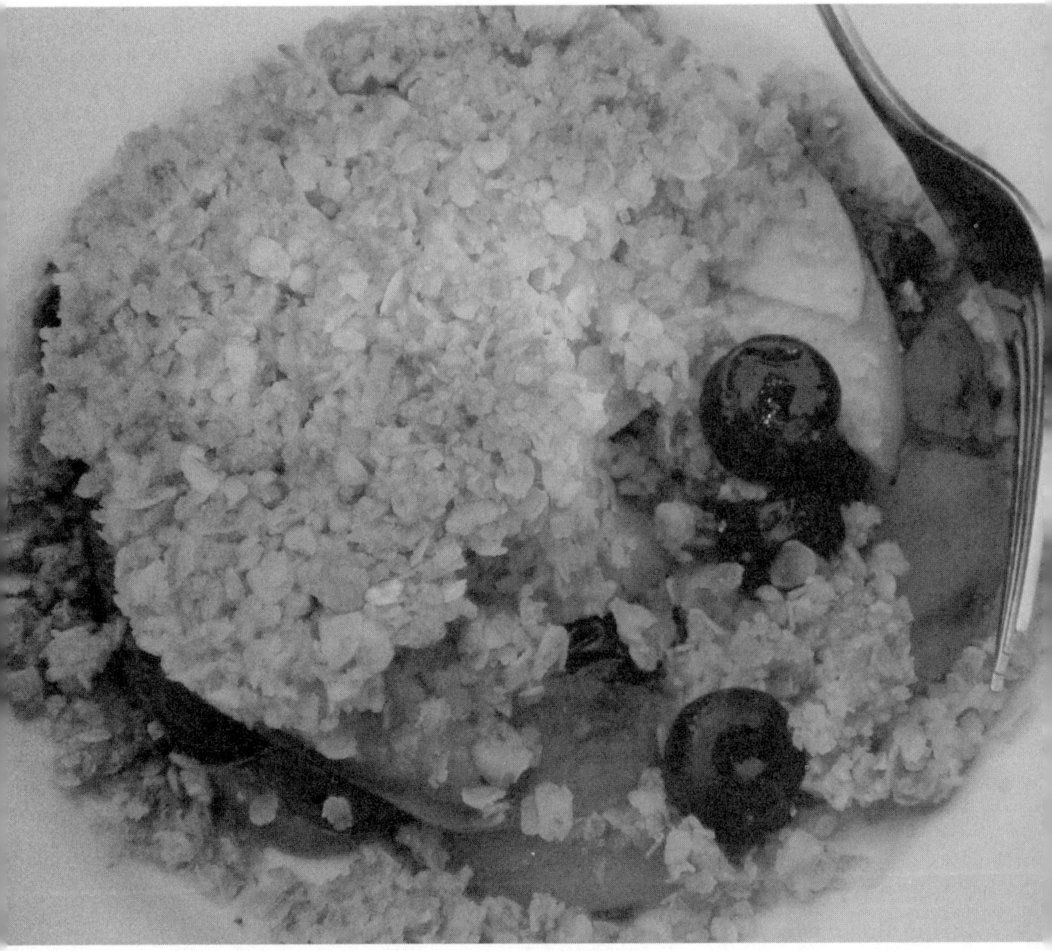

Blueberry Nectarine Crunch

¼ cup fresh blueberries
2 fresh nectarines, sliced thin
1 tablespoon honey
¼ cup quick-cook oats
⅛ cup natural sugar (sugar in the raw)
2 teaspoons whole-wheat flour
4 teaspoons Spectrum Spread (butter replacement)

Preheat oven to 375°. In a medium bowl toss fresh blueberries and nectarines with honey. Set aside. In another medium bowl use your hands to combine oats, sugar, flour, and spectrum spread until mixture forms a course texture.

In a small oven ready pie pan, layer nectarine slices around bottom and sides, fill the center with fresh blueberries and top with oat mixture. Bake approximately ten to fifteen minutes until top is golden brown. Serves two.

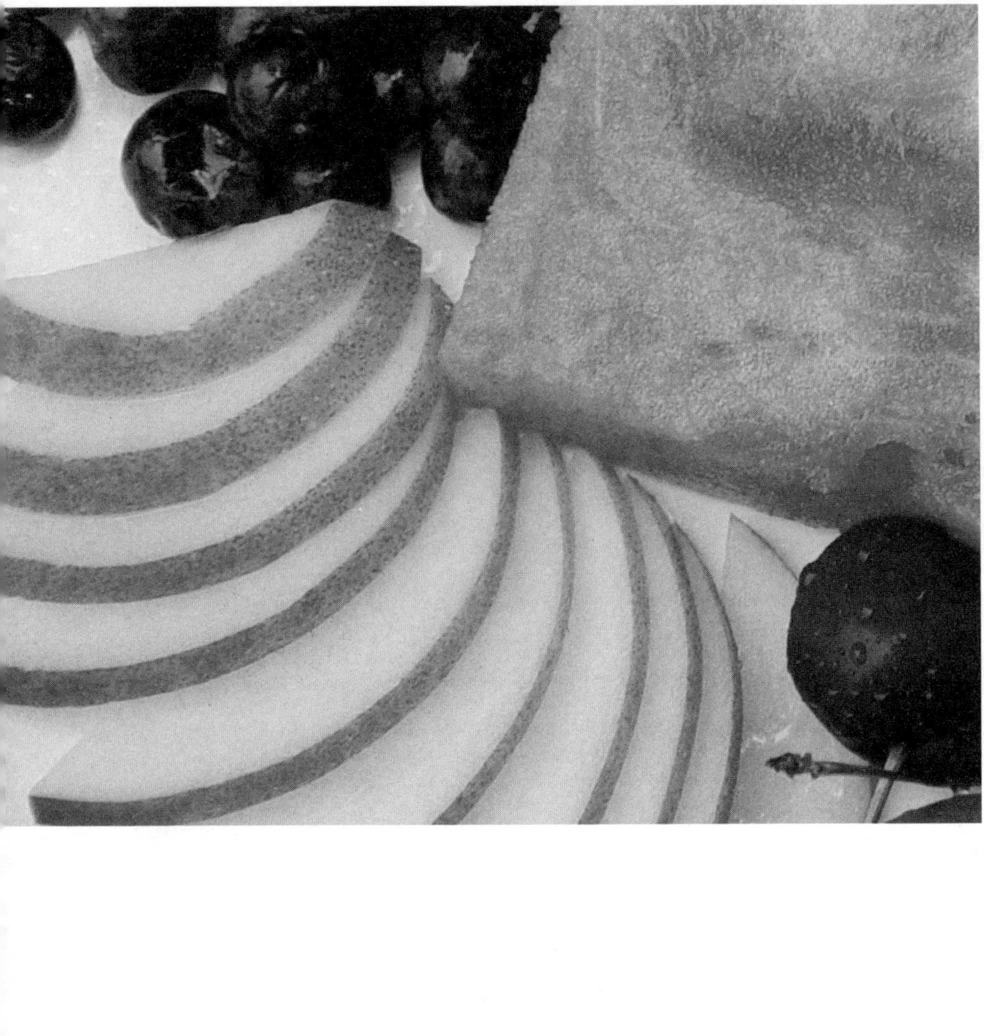

Eating in Balance

Every meal is an opportunity to get on the right track. Proper eating schedules, menus, quality choices, and portion control are the foundation for overall health. Make this one of the most proactive areas of your life by learning the basics of nutrition. Your body and the other people you influence with food choices will be lifelong beneficiaries of this immeasurable education and balanced eating program.

And now a word on . . .

Drugs, Tobacco, Caffeine, and Alcohol

Enough has been said about the ill effects of these substances, so I just want to make a short pitch. If you are using any of the above, please do whatever it takes to stop them now. Seek help if you need it. If you have children or influence them, be sure to set the example early and educate them aggressively on the ill effects of these choices.

Housecleaning

In addition to food, housecleaning products can contribute to an unhealthy environment in your home. It's scary to read the back of most products at the grocery store. The warnings and directions for use make it clear that the ingredients are extremely harmful. Here again we sacrifice health for convenience. They boast quick, easy, and no-scrubbing features, but the residual effects from the fumes and gases they emit can be damaging to your body. Most products suggest adequate ventilation, rubber gloves, and a mask during application. How many bathrooms don't even have a window? Who uses a mask? We ignore these warnings and continue to use these products because it's easy and they do the job thoroughly and quickly.

Do your health a favor and don't contribute any more harmful pollution to yourself, your family, or your home. Use natural cleaning products to detoxify your home and eliminate the offensive odors. Go through all of the cans and bottles under your sink and in your closets and throw away the chemical agents. Natural products are available in most stores and easily replace your existing ones. You may need to scrub a little harder or a little longer, but the short- and long-term effects on your health are worth the effort.

20/20 Vision —

SUGGESTED CLEANING PRODUCTS

▶ Use a citrus-based all-purpose cleaner for most jobs. It smells great, works great, and isn't harmful to you, your family, or your home.

▶ Use a vinegar-and-water mixture to clean windows.

▶ Mix a natural dishwashing soap and water in a spray bottle to spray on your houseplants. It will leave them shiny and avoid dust build up.

▶ Use nonchlorine bleach on your clothes.

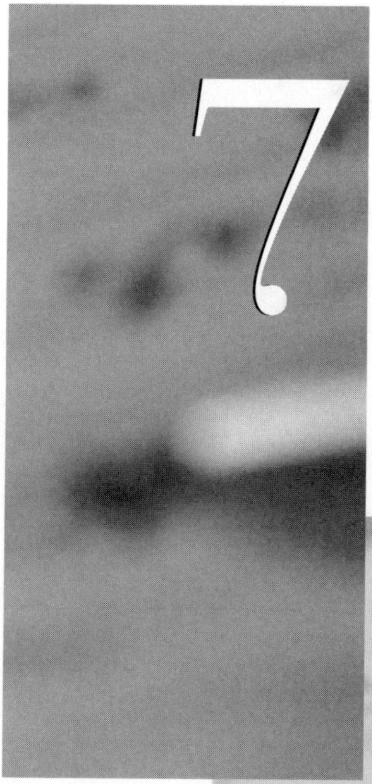

7 Taking Care of Business

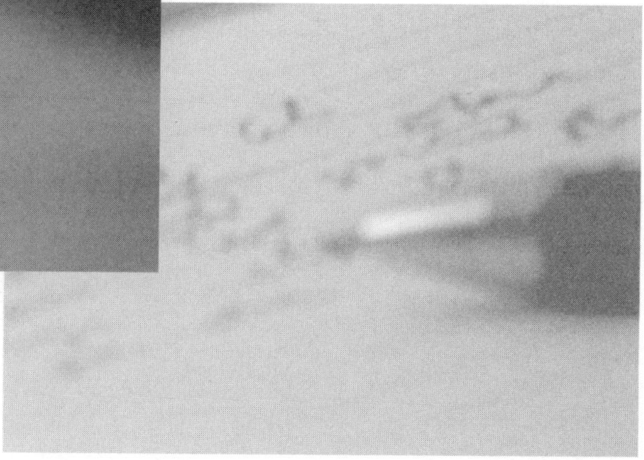

THE BUSINESS TEST

A. Never = 1 point
B. Sometimes = 2 points
C. Always = 3 points

1. Are you inspired by your profession? ____

2. Do you give your job the best of you? ____

3. Do you develop a blueprint for your career path? ____

4. Do you update your knowledge of your profession through regular training? ____

5. Do you control the time you spend working? ____

6. Do you have an organized system for personal files, documents, and finances? ____

7. Are you on time for appointments and do you meet deadlines? ____

8. Do you budget for your personal living expenses? ____

9. Do you evaluate your financial needs for the future? ____

10. Do you clean out your personal clutter? ____

Scoring

Write your score next to each question number and then total.

1. _____
2. _____
3. _____
4. _____
5. _____
6. _____
7. _____
8. _____
9. _____
10. _____

Total: _____

Evaluation

10–15: It's time to reevaluate and take small steps to get on the path to achieving balance in this area.

16–20: You're on the path to balance in this pillar. Focus on your weak areas and you will take noticeable positive steps.

21–30: Congratulations! You're living at a high level of balance in this pillar. Determine the areas that will have the greatest impact on enhancing your life experiences.

As I mentioned in the introduction, I include Business as the final Pillar of Life Balance because so much of our time is devoted to it and what we do for work is so much a part of who we are. It would be foolish to write a book about balance without addressing this area, which is so often one of the prime places where we lose our balance. You'll recall that when I say Business, I mean both work and personal business.

Simply put, if your career is consuming all your waking hours, you will never achieve balance in the other pillars. You may not think you have the power to change much about your work life, but you do. Not only is change necessary for a healthy present but, as they say, at the end of your life you are not going to wish you had spent more time at the office. You may well regret missing your kid play a rooster in the Thanksgiving Festival.

Then there's our personal business, which consists of our finances, home, medical, insurance, auto, and so on. Without an organized system, managing the paperwork alone can take up all our "free" time. Personal business can easily throw our lives out of balance.

Making Your Work Work for You

Mitch was working in sales for a software company and made average money for someone in his position. He wasn't getting rich, but he had a wife and two children and the job benefits were good. Mitch craved more. He worked hard and felt the benefits were going to the company and not him. He decided that the time was now to take the leap. His kids were young and he could always go back and find a job if he had to. He took the $4,000 he had in his savings account and started his own business. Within two years he tripled his salary and now owns a very successful company.

Many of us view our career choice simply as "work." We view the fact that we have to earn money to survive in this society as a necessary evil and choose or stay in careers that just provide a paycheck and nothing more. We follow in the family business, take a job through some connection, or follow our college major. We begin to make money, incur expenses that set our standard of living, and settle into a financial lifestyle. The fear of changing jobs or starting over with no money threatens this lifestyle and prevents us from taking an inspirational career path. Is that it? Are we done? Are we stuck once we choose?

Remember, you will spend more time at work than anywhere else, so your choice of what to do will affect your whole outlook toward life. That's why I urge you to take the time to make informed and educated choices that will provide stimulation and the financial security you need.

There are countless professions and businesses available to all of us. If you desire more from your profession, you need to go after it now. Continually conduct your own research and learn about professions that interest you and will elevate your professional life. The advantage we have in this society is the ability to choose. You may not find your perfect job right out of school, or if you are in the workplace you may not find the perfect job right after your current job. There are no rules that you must make a decision and stick with it for the rest of your life, so always view your choices as steps to the perfect career. Enroll in career counseling classes, go to franchise seminars, take part-time jobs, or volunteer as an intern in a company within the industry you are attracted to.

The key word in your hunt is passion. Your career practically defines who you are. In many cases it gives people self-worth as well as a place to go in the morning. Don't settle and let it be just that. Pick a path that makes you jump out of bed in the morning. Don't dream it, be it.

Of course it's never easy to leave a good-paying job, profession, or business, even in the pursuit of passion. That being said, you can never recover lost time doing something you hate. If you are in a business just for money, chances are you will never make enough to give you the financial freedom you desire. There are always alternatives, and it will take sacrifices and creativity, but do not forfeit professional excitement

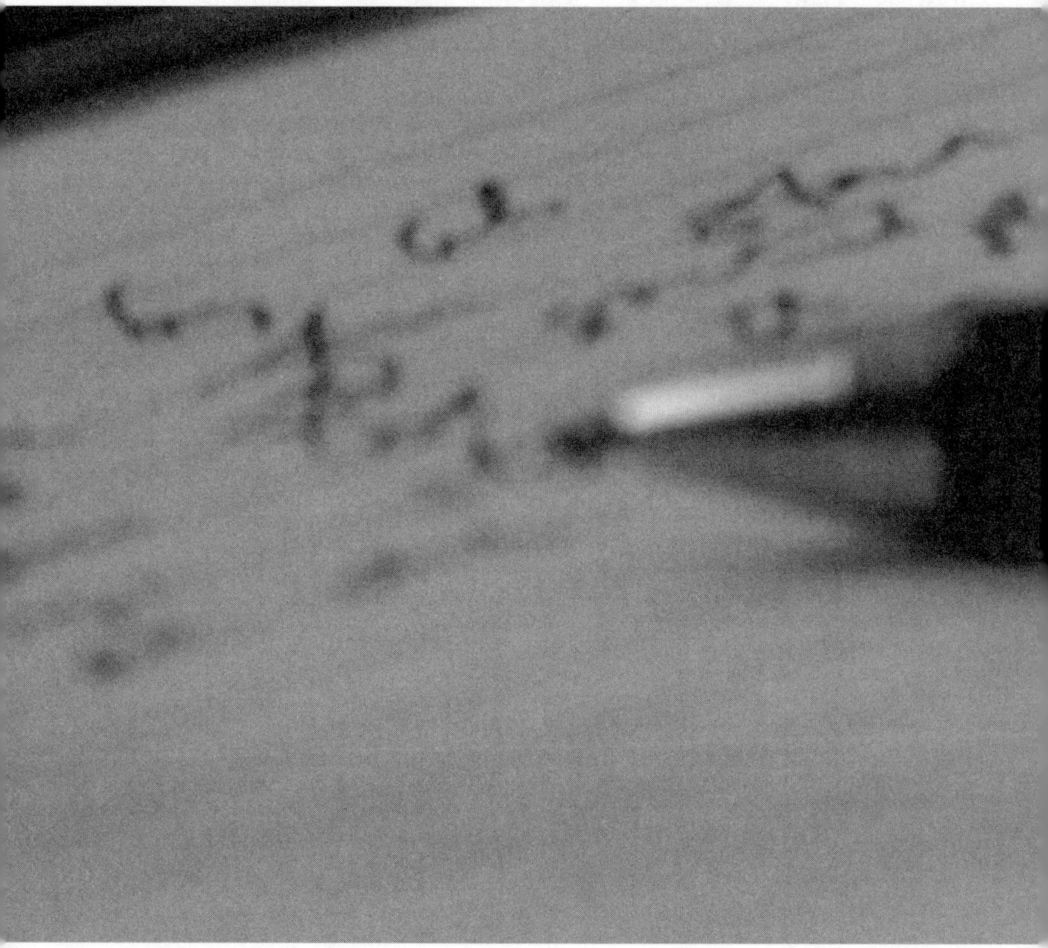

and enthusiasm just for money. Love the pursuit and the rewards will follow.

If you are in a career that *does* inspire you, be sure to continue your education and reinvent yourself. Don't allow yourself to become complacent and ignore change and innovation. Every industry is going through technological and financial changes, and you should be ahead of the curve in order to maintain pace with your colleagues and new hires. Take advantage of company benefits that pay for related education and seminars. Strive to be "of" something, not just "in" it.

Before you make any changes in your work life, reflect on what you want and need from work and where it fits into your overall life plan, because your overall goals will dictate the choices you pursue. If you are already in a career that is working reasonably well for you, try to be as productive as you can within the workday. Living with urgency and focused direction all day should allow you to accomplish your professional day and still leave you the hours you need to balance out the rest of your life.

20/20 Vision—

ACTIVITIES FOR CAREER EVALUATION

▶ Make a list of all aspects of a career that are important to you. Prioritize them in order of importance and use this as a yardstick to evaluate all your career choices. Update this as you grow in your professional maturity, but make it your personal set of standards by which you live your career.

▶ Look at all of your expenses and know your minimum financial requirements. Don't take on any expense that will force you over your comfort level.

▶ Prepare a professional time schedule. Put entries in your calendar that set limits on the time you want to give to your daily career time. Use this as incentive to either work more efficiently or to pursue a new career that fits this timetable.

▶ Take a seminar that will enhance your knowledge or abilities.

▶ When interviewing for a job, be sure to interview your prospective employer. This is as much a move for you as it is for them. Make a list of questions pertaining to responsibilities, growth potential, time commitments, education and training benefits, and culture. Being proactive in an interview shows your commitment to making quality choices in your life.

The Life Balance System
for Organizing Your Personal Business

You will always have bills to pay, mail and/or e-mail to read and evaluate, expiration dates to keep track of, and paperwork to fill out. Having personal business is just a fact of life. The key to balance is in having a system to manage this process. If you tend to miss deadlines, make late payments, forget renewals, or lose documents, you are actually giving away precious time to *mismanagement*. We are all guilty of this at some point in our lives, but a good system can minimize or eliminate these occurrences and bring this critical area of our lives into balance with the others.

I developed the following system to help you organize your paperwork, finances, e-mail, and due dates. I use it myself. It will eliminate all those unruly piles and the stress of having to remember what's in them and what needs to be done when. It will allow you to keep your mind clear and give you the mental freedom to devote to the rest of your life—in balance.

Tools

In order to begin the process of creating an effective system you will need to gather some basic tools:

- ▶ A file cabinet
- ▶ A fireproof safe
- ▶ Your planner (see chapter 1)
- ▶ A financial software program or a file-based "tickler" system
- ▶ A word processing program or a paper-based document system

A good office supply store will have all of these things. They can be pricey, but consider that mostly they are one-time expenses, well worth it in the long run.

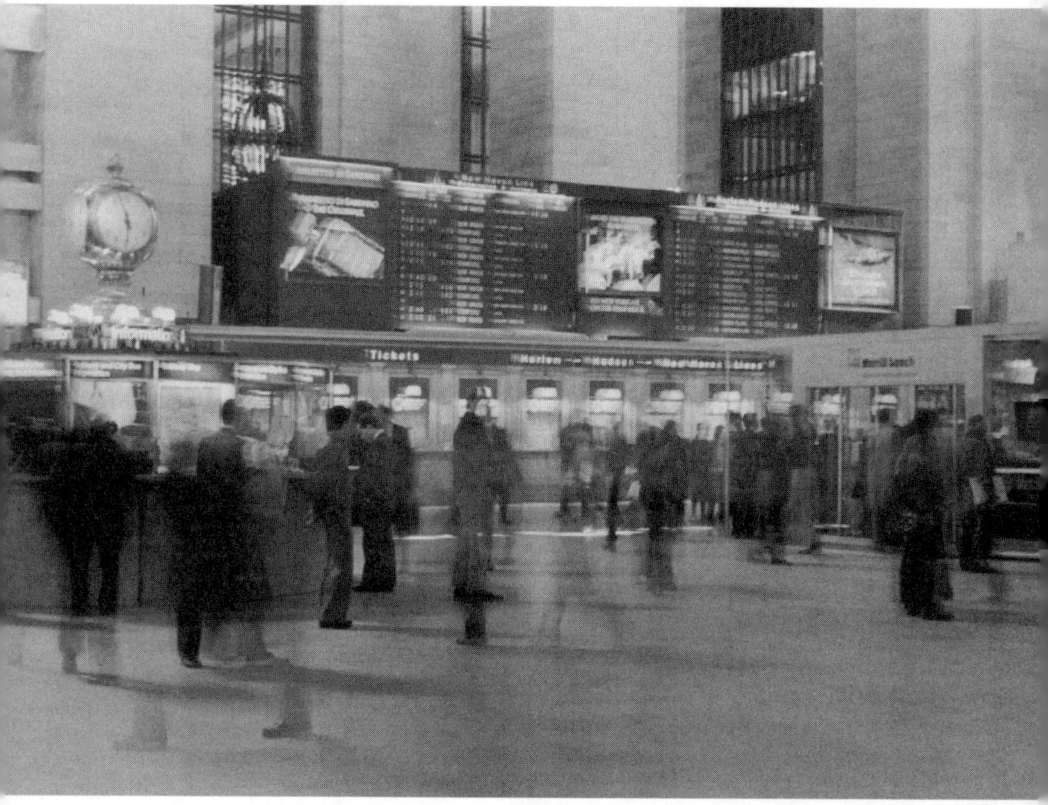
Tickets

The File Cabinet

A file cabinet can help you get rid of all your piles. No, not by giving you a place to hide all the piles but as a first step toward creating a file system so you won't have to create all those vexing piles in the first place.

The Fireproof Safe

Some documents are irreplaceable or difficult to replace. These critically important papers should be stored in a fireproof safe. Get one that's big enough to hold hanging files so the papers in the safe are organized and easily accessible when you need them.

The Planner

Utilize your planner's task list and appointment calendar for entering renewal dates on policies and due dates for memberships, registrations, and so on. Enter recurring appointments, such as auto inspections and annual physicals.

Financial Software

A financial software program can be invaluable to getting your personal business in balance. Quicken® and Money® are the most popular and more than sufficient. If you are not computer based, I will offer a paper file system as well.

Word Processing Software

Any simple word processing program will do. If you do not use a computer, a notebook is sufficient.

20/20 VISION —

ACTIVITIES TO TAKE CONTROL OF YOUR PERSONAL BUSINESS

Finances

Finances include banking and bill paying, financial planning, and taxes.

Step 1: Clean house.

▶ Go through all your financial paperwork. Decide what's important and keep it. Get rid of all the promotional literature and tons of extra envelopes you have accumulated.

▶ Review your credit cards and cancel the accounts that are draining you. Also review the percentage rate you are paying and the rewards program. There are many cards available today, and they vary widely in terms of rates and rewards. Go online to compare features and rates at *Quicken.com* and *Bankrate.com*.

Step 2: Create files.

▶ The first set of files you should make is your bill file. Create a "Bills to Pay" file and a second set of files for paid bills and stubs organized by category. Examples include "Telephone," "Mortgage," "Auto Insurance," and so on. This provides easy access to records if you need to refer back to them. If you pay bills manually, organize the pay stubs by the due date in the "Bills to Pay" file and put the receipt portions in their own separate category file. If you use financial software and/or online banking, enter all of your bills into the software and file the entire bill in its own separate category file. (With online banking, recurring bills with fixed amounts can be paid automatically on specified dates, e.g. the first day of the month or quarter, the fourth Friday of the month, etc.)

- Create a set of files for all your banking records including deposit slips, statements, and cancelled checks.

- Create a set of files for all investments and financial planning documents.

- Create a file for all tax-related documents. If you take deductions, create a file for tax-related receipts and enter the item, category, date, and amount in your financial software or a notebook for easy totaling at the end of the year.

Step 3: Schedule recurring tasks.

- **Paying bills.** Create a monthly budget to keep expenses within your comfort range and update as needed. Schedule recurring bill-paying days in your planner. Twice a month is sufficient. Use your folder, software, and/or online banking service to schedule the days to make payments.

- **Investments and financial planning.** Schedule as a recurring task a review of your investments and financial-planning goals, such as retirement and college savings plans. Check with your financial advisor about when and how often these reviews should take place.

- **Taxes.** Schedule an annual recurring task to organize your tax documents.

- **Clean-out day.** Schedule an annual recurring task for each January to clean out all of your financial files and put them in a large expanding file folder. Mark the year clearly on the front and put the file in a financial storage box. Mark the outside of the storage box with the dates of the files inside for easy access. The suggested term for keeping personal financial records is seven years.

Home Management and Possessions

Step 1: Clean house.

Our minds are a reflection of our surroundings. If you are a pack rat and live in a cluttered mess, then chances are your mind is not free to think clearly. Here are some suggestions for cleaning house.

▶ Clean out your closets, garage, or any other place where you hide stuff. Get rid of clothes you will never wear or possessions that take up space. Donate them to a local charity. In some instances they are tax deductible. Do this when you are feeling especially unsentimental and motivated. You are never going to fit into or wear that pastel pantsuit again. Just let it go.

▶ Clean out your cupboards and refrigerator and get rid of dated and unhealthy food. Keep lists of all of the food you throw away to avoid spending money wastefully on it again.

▶ Have an extra set of keys made and hide them outside your house and/or give a set to a neighbor, friend, or relative that lives close by.

Step 2: Create files.

▶ Create a set of files for all your important home documents. Your mortgage papers, deed, lease, insurance, and so on. Put these in the fireproof safe.

▶ Create a set of files for the instruction manuals for all the items you own. Create files by category, such as appliances, electronics, cameras, computers, and power tools.

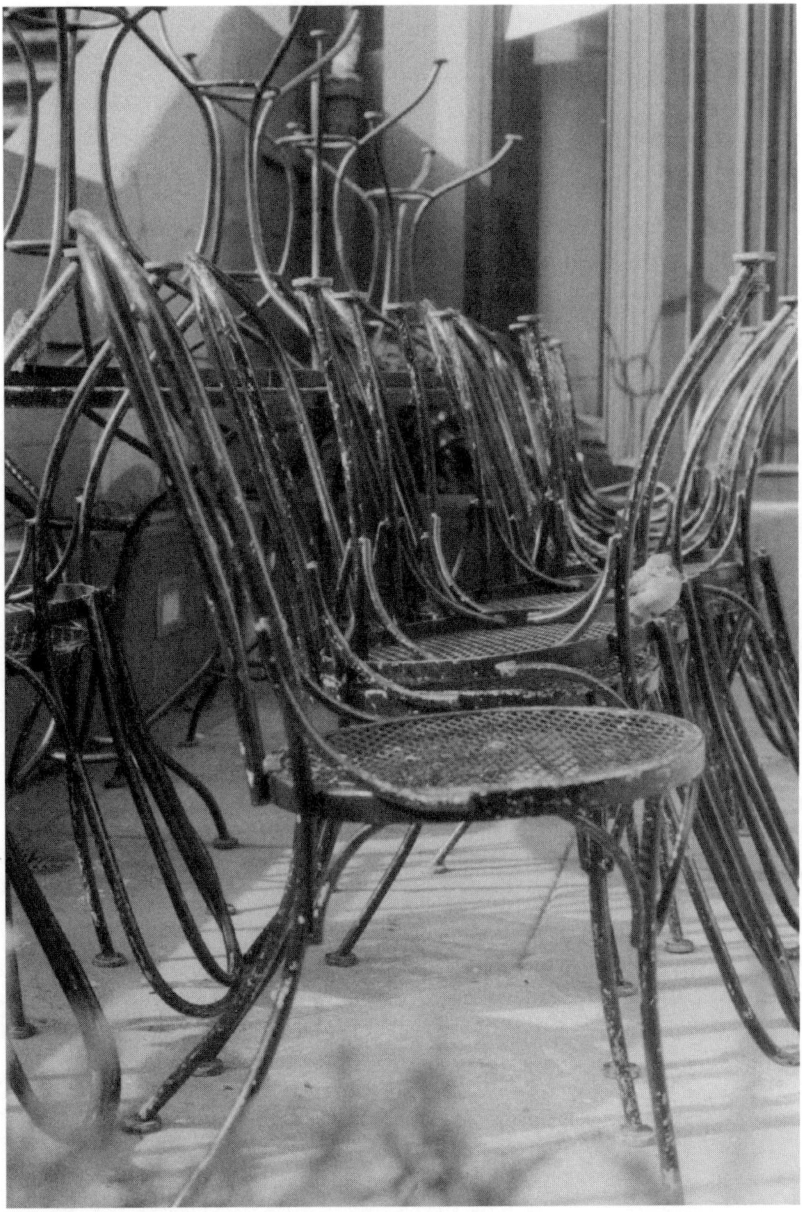

▶ Create a duplicate set of category files for the corresponding warranties and receipts for the items.

▶ Organize your photos into albums or boxes and label them. Spend a little time and money on this. Ten years from now you may look back and wish you had taken better care of your sentimental images.

▶ Organize your videotapes by numbering them and creating a document (electronic or in a notebook) with the number, title, date, and brief description of each event captured.

Step 3: Schedule recurring tasks.

▶ Set an annual recurring task to review your homeowner's insurance policy to evaluate any improvements or additional possessions that may need to be added. In addition, videotape your home and possessions and store the tape in your fireproof safe in the event it is needed for insurance purposes.

▶ Set recurring tasks for home maintenance projects.

○ The clean-out: go through every room, closet, garage, and shed and throw away the clutter.

○ Schedule maintenance on major equipment such as air conditioners, heating units, refrigerators, stoves, pools, and so on. Go through your home, make a list, and set up the projects in your planner.

○ Schedule tasks for gardening, gutters, painting, and so on.

Medical

Step 1: Clean house.
Get rid of outdated insurance policies, unnecessary documents, and old, expired prescription medicines.

Step 2: Create files.

▶ Create a file for all policies and doctor information.

▶ Create a file for all receipts, procedures, and records.

▶ Create a log (electronic or in a notebook) of all procedures and serious illnesses by date and practitioner.

▶ Enter all of your doctors' and specialists' names, addresses, and categories into your address book. File them by category as well to allow for easy recall.

Step 3: Schedule recurring tasks.

▶ Set up a recurring reminder to schedule an annual, complete checkup. Make and keep the appointment.

▶ Set an annual recurring task to review your benefit plan for adequate coverage.

Insurance

Step 1: Clean house.
Find a good insurance broker and have her or him work up a quote for your home, auto, and life insurance needs. Be sure to advise your broker of any items of extra value that may need to be scheduled separately.

Step 2: Create files.
Create separate files for all policies and store them in the fireproof safe.

Step 3: Schedule recurring tasks.
Set an annual recurring task to review your policies for adequate coverage.

Auto

Step 1: Clean house.

▶ Our cars are another popular place where junk easily accumulates. Don't let your car contribute to your clutter. Keep it clean inside and out.

▶ Make an extra set of keys.

Step 2: Create files.

▶ Create separate files for all loan documents, titles, and insurance policies. Store them in the fireproof safe.

▶ Keep a maintenance log (electronic or in a notebook).

Step 3: Schedule recurring tasks.

▶ Set a recurring task for regular maintenance—oil, tune up, tires, and so on.

▶ Set a task for renewing inspection and registration.

Information Management

Step 1: Clean house.

▶ Throw away old magazines and newspapers that you will never read.

▶ Clean out your e-mail folders and other documents stored on your computer.

Step 2: Create files.

▶ Create a "to-read" file. When you open up your mail or receive paper in any manner, read it, throw it away, or file it in the appropriate folder. If you don't have the time to read it immediately, file it in the to-read file.

▶ Create an electronic or paper document that lists all of your critical information. Include your credit card numbers, contents of your wallet, social security numbers, and birth dates. In case anything is stolen or missing, you can access this information easily.

▶ Create a file for all your personal information items, including passports, birth certificates, social security cards, and other membership identification cards you don't carry in your wallet.

▶ Deal with your e-mail! Having a long list of e-mails in your inbox contributes to information overload. Deal with e-mails immediately or create separate folders and file them under the appropriate categories.

Step 3: Schedule recurring tasks.

► Schedule a weekly recurring task to go through the to-read file.

► Create a monthly recurring task to clean out your e-mail folders.

► Create an annual recurring task to update your critical information document.

Hobbies and Travel

Step 1: Clean house.

Get rid of all the toys you never use anymore. Donate them to charity, hold a garage sale, or advertise them for sale online or in your local paper.

Step 2: Create files.

▶ Hobby: Create a file for all ideas that relate to your hobby. For example, if your hobby is painting, file inspirational pictures that portray a place or technique you want to paint.

▶ Travel: Create a file of interesting places you would like to visit. Keep brochures or articles so you can refer to the file when you are deciding on your next adventure.

Step 3: Schedule recurring tasks.

▶ Set a recurring task to review your hobby file and travel file.

▶ Set a recurring task to make your travel plans!

The personal business in your life can be overwhelming if it's not organized. As our society becomes more computerized, we seem to accumulate even more paper and information to control. By having a system set up to manage the flow and accessibility of this information, you will streamline the energy and time it takes to handle it. The results will offer you more time to enjoy balance in the more inspirational aspects of your life.

As you begin to balance your life, remember that regardless of your personality, you need to take care of business. What you choose to do to earn a living and your ability to stay organized personally are intertwined as the necessary cornerstones for thriving in balance. Keeping work in balance requires an organized approach that stems from your personal organization. Keeping your personal business in balance requires a work life that allows time and energy to achieve it. If you focus on these areas of business, you will find relief from the heavy weight that can hold you back from a worry-free pursuit of a life in balance.

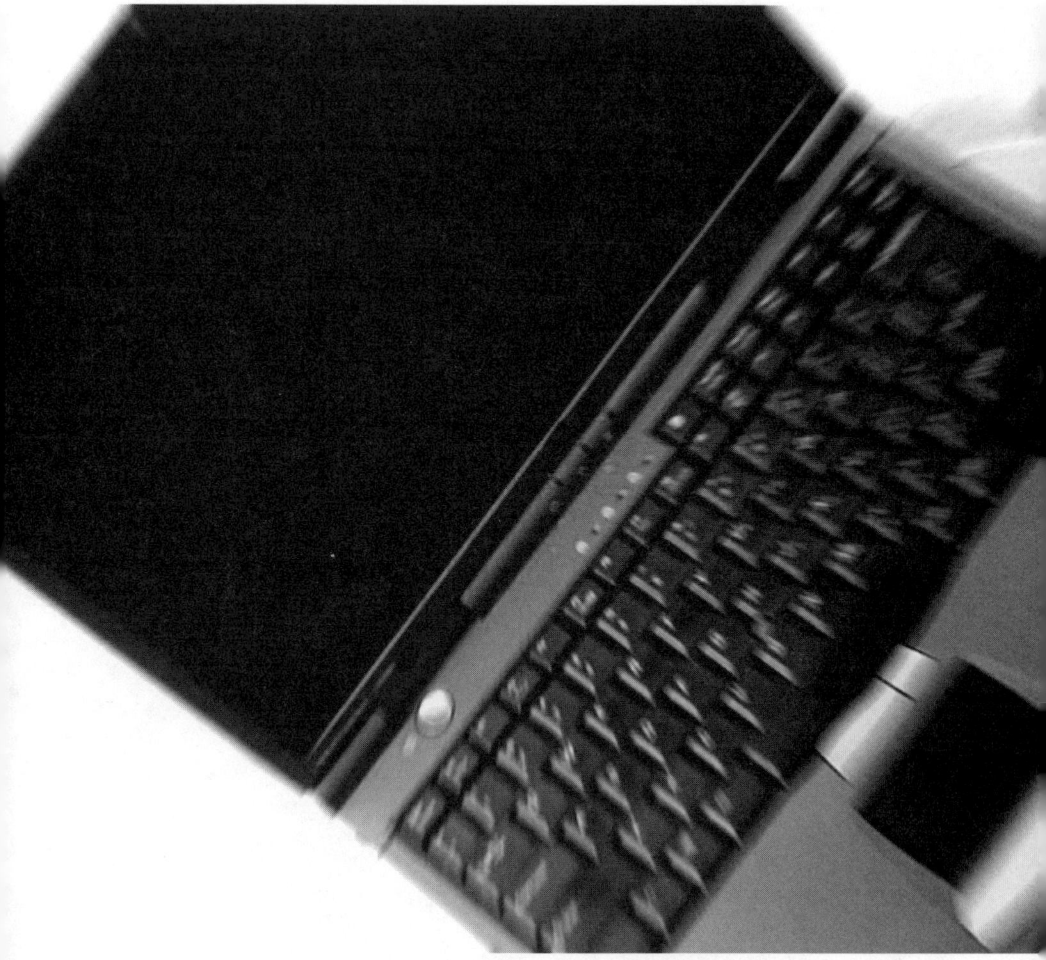

In Conclusion:

BALANCE FOR LIFE

As you have read through these pages you have seen that balance is an ongoing journey that is achieved through an organized system and a heightened awareness of the value we place on the various important elements in our life. My goal was to share what I have learned and achieved in these areas, the way in which I continue to experience them, and the inspiration I receive daily from living in pretty good balance. My hope is that you can achieve balanced living by applying the techniques and by recognizing the value in areas that you may be neglecting or have never considered. Perhaps you are already starting to reap the benefits.

There is a tremendous amount of pain and suffering in this world, and you may be in the middle of it or a close bystander. If not now, it is a certainty that you will experience suffering in your life. We all do. That is precisely why we have no time to waste creating, experiencing, or contributing to the negative aspects of life. It is time to take the high road in all situations and adopt an elevated set of standards to live by.

My philosophy is simple: We don't need to grow old, we can grow young by continually learning, creating, and reinventing ourselves. We don't need to follow history by finding ourselves at the end of our lives saying, "Everything is clear to me now, and if I could do it all over again, I would . . ." The world will not stop for you to get it together. By the time you are ready to enjoy life it may be too late. Initiate small steps now toward living in balance. Push yourself to find the wisdom and foresight to make it happen today.

A life in balance may seem far off, but every small change can bring you closer. Clear your thoughts and create your own blueprint for the biography you want to see. We never know what the road ahead has in store for us, but it is our choice on how to get there.

And remember, achieving balance in your life is not something you do just for you. We all have an effect on the people around us. As you change the way you live, you will inspire others to change, too. You will become more sensitive to their struggles and want to make a difference in their lives, because it isn't enough to achieve just for the sake of achieving. Part of achieving balance means bringing other people up around you. That is a gift that can't be bought at the mall.

For the most part you'll inspire people just by your presence; your attitude and sense of well-being will begin to rub off. And that is both an awesome feeling and a great responsibility. You will be a living example of a deep commitment and passion for living.

If you are a parent, seize the opportunity to help your children learn the power of balance. The business sector aspects of my Life Balance Plan may not be as important to young children, but all the others play a key role, even in the lives of toddlers. Helping your kids prioritize what is important to them and live by their values is one of the greatest gifts you can give. Keep tabs on how much time your family is spending on activities, television, video games, sports, and schoolwork, and help them understand that all these activities contributes to a well-balanced life. Modeling balance is the best way to instill in them a sense of healthy priorities, self-confidence, and an increased sensitivity to the world around them.

And finally, strange as it sounds, I want you to write your own obituary. First write the one that describes the life you have led and are continuing to lead today. If it's not what you want to be remembered for, write another one describing the person you want to be. Now start living that life today.

These are days you will remember and every day is another entry into your own life story. You build on each occurrence and set in stone the memories of who and what you were. If they ever make your movie, will you want to see it?

To Our Readers

Red Wheel, an imprint of Red Wheel/Weiser, publishes books on topics ranging from spunky self-help, spirituality, personal growth, and relationships to women's issues and social issues. Our mission is to publish quality books that will make a difference in people's lives—how we feel about ourselves and how we relate to one another and to the world at large. We value integrity, compassion, and receptivity, both in the books we publish and in the way we do business.

Our readers are our most important resource, and we value your input, suggestions, and ideas about what you would like to see published. Please feel free to contact us, to request our latest book catalog, or to be added to our mailing list.

Red Wheel/Weiser, LLC
P.O. Box 612
York Beach, ME 03910-0612
www.redwheelweiser.com

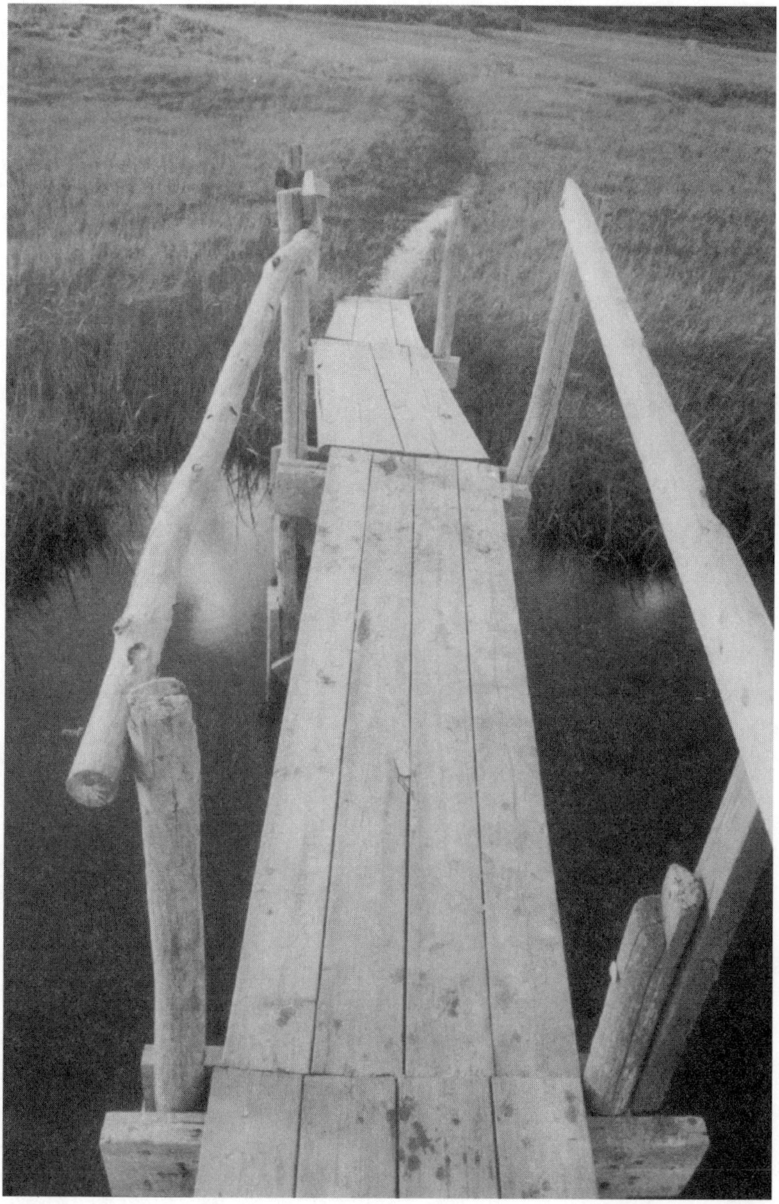